D1129597

INDICATORS OF BUSINESS EXPANSIONS AND CONTRACTIONS

OCCASIONAL PAPER 103

GEOFFREY H. MOORE
NATIONAL BUREAU OF ECONOMIC RESEARCH
JULIUS SHISKIN
BUREAU OF THE CENSUS

INDICATORS OF BUSINESS EXPANSIONS AND CONTRACTIONS

NATIONAL BUREAU OF ECONOMIC RESEARCH
NEW YORK 1967
Distributed by
COLUMBIA UNIVERSITY PRESS
NEW YORK AND LONDON

Library of Congress Catalog Card Number 66-30650
Printed in the United States of America

The choice before man is not whether to engage in forecasting or to abstain from it, but whether to base expectations on 'hunches' or on lessons carefully distilled from experience.

ARTHUR F. BURNS
The Frontiers of Economic Knowledge

Relation of the Directors to the Work and Publications of the National Bureau of Economic Research

1. The object of the National Bureau of Economic Research is to ascertain and to present to the public important economic facts and their interpretation in a scientific and impartial manner. The Board of Directors is charged with the responsibility of ensuring that the work of the National Bureau is carried on in strict conformity with this object.

2. To this end the Board of Directors shall appoint one or more Directors of Research.

3. The Director or Directors of Research shall submit to the members of the Board, or to its Executive Committee, for their formal adoption, all specific proposals concerning researches to be instituted.

4. No report shall be published until the Director or Directors of Research shall have submitted to the Board a summary drawing attention to the character of the data and their utilization in the report, the nature and treatment of the problems involved, the main conclusions, and such other information as in their opinion would serve to determine the suitability of the report for publication in accordance with the principles of the National Bureau.

5. A copy of any manuscript proposed for publication shall also be submitted to each member of the Board. For each manuscript to be so submitted a special committee shall be appointed by the President, or at his designation by the Executive Director, consisting of three Directors selected as nearly as may be one from each general division of the Board. The names of the special manuscript committee shall be stated to each Director when the summary and report described in paragraph (4) are sent to him. It shall be the duty of each member of the committee to read the manuscript. If each member of the special committee signifies his approval within thirty days, the manuscript may be published. If each member of the special committee has not signified his approval within thirty days of the transmittal of the report and manuscript, the Director of Research shall then notify each member of the Board, requesting approval or disapproval of publication, and thirty additional days shall be granted for this purpose. The manuscript shall then not be published unless at least a majority of the entire Board and a two-thirds majority of those members of the Board who shall have voted on the proposal within the time fixed for the receipt of votes on the publication proposed shall have approved.

6. No manuscript may be published, though approved by each member of the special committee, until forty-five days have elapsed from the transmittal of the summary and report. The interval is allowed for the receipt of any memorandum of dissent or reservation, together with a brief statement of his reasons, that any member may wish to express; and such memorandum of dissent or reservation shall be published with the manuscript if he so desires. Publication does not, however, imply that each member of the Board has read the manuscript, or that either members of the Board in general, or of the special committee, have passed upon its validity in every detail.

7. A copy of this resolution shall, unless otherwise determined by the Board, be printed in each copy of every National Bureau book.

(Resolution adopted October 25, 1926, as revised February 6, 1933, and February 24, 1941)

Contents

Tables

Charts

Acknowledgments

An empirical investigation of this scope has to be the work of many persons. The authors owe much to the advisers who counseled them. Arthur F. Burns was virtually a collaborator in the enterprise, and his constructive ideas influenced every part of the project. The innovations in the treatment of indicators had to be tested against the critical minds of other investigators before they could be made public. This contribution was made by our colleagues, Victor Zarnowitz, Ilse Mintz, and Edgar Fiedler; by members of a committee appointed by the American Economic Association to advise the Census Bureau on *Business Cycle Developments,* especially Donald J. Daly, Gottfried Haberler, Bert G. Hickman, Frank E. Morris, Lawrence R. Klein, and Beryl W. Sprinkel; and by Leonard H. Lempert and Gordon W. McKinley. Numerous modifications of our plans and manuscript drafts were made upon their suggestions and criticisms.

During the three years over which this study was carried out, the technical skill and devotion of Sophie Sakowitz, Johanna Stern, Dorothy O'Brien, and Esther Reichner were unequaled. Their patience in redoing the work several times, after experience had indicated flaws in earlier plans, is a quality that, unfortunately, will remain undetected by the reader, though greatly appreciated by the authors. We are indebted, also, to James F. McRee, Jr., for editing the manuscript.

This monograph is part of a comprehensive study conducted by the National Bureau to evaluate and improve short-term forecasts of aggregate economic activity. The study was aided by grants to the National Bureau from Whirlpool Corporation, General Electric Company, Ford Motor Company Fund, U.S. Steel Corporation, and the Relm Foundation. A grant of electronic computer time to the National Bureau by the International Business Machines Corporation was used for some of the statistical analyses in this report.

Mr. Shiskin carried out his part of the research while on leave from the Bureau of the Census, and the Census Bureau is not to be held responsible for any of the statements made.

I

Introduction and Summary

The National Bureau of Economic Research published its first list of business cycle indicators in 1938.[1] Compiled by Wesley C. Mitchell and Arthur F. Burns, the list was based upon a study of nearly 500 monthly or quarterly series covering varying historical periods, but ending with the business cycle that reached its trough in 1933. They selected the 21 "most trustworthy" indicators of cyclical revival, and presented a fuller list of 71 series that "have been tolerably consistent in their timing in relation to business cycle revivals and at the same time of sufficiently general interest to warrant some attention by students of current economic conditions."

About a dozen years later a second comprehensive review was made.[2] The new study was based upon a larger number of series, about 800, and utilized measures of cyclical behavior through 1938. This study went beyond the earlier report in several ways: indicators of recession as well as of revival were covered; probability standards against which the historical records of timing and conformity could be judged were introduced; a comprehensive economic classification of the 800 series was used in making the final selection of indicators; and the selected series were classified into three categories reflecting their timing at business cycle peaks and troughs: leading, roughly coincident, and lagging. The final 21 series selected included 8 leading series, 8 roughly coincident series, and 5 lagging series.

This list was again revised in 1960.[3] The new list was based upon a still larger number of series and upon business cycle measures through 1958. Some series in the 1950 list were dropped and some new series were added; as a result 26 indicators were selected, including 12 leading series, 9 roughly coincident, and 5 lagging. A supplementary list of additional series was also shown.

In the fall of 1957, at the request of the chairman of the Council of Economic Advisers, Raymond J. Saulnier, the Bureau of the Census started a research program to develop a monthly report on indicators that would take advantage of new findings about the relations of economic processes over time, the availability of a great many economic time series in seasonally adjusted form, and large-scale electronic computing facilities. Close working relations between the Council of Economic Advisers, the Bureau of the Census, and the National Bureau of Economic Research were maintained throughout the developmental stages of this report. After some four years of experimentation and testing, the Bureau of the Census began publishing the report in October 1961 under the title *Business Cycle Developments,* and a description of its history and methods was published by the National Bureau that same month.[4]

The monthly report has shown the 1960 NBER list of 26 indicators as well as 54 additional U.S. series, or 80 in all. Of these, 30 are

[1] Wesley C. Mitchell and Arthur F. Burns, *Statistical Indicators of Cyclical Revivals,* Bulletin 69, New York, National Bureau of Economic Research, May 28, 1938. Reprinted in Geoffrey H. Moore (ed.), *Business Cycle Indicators,* Princeton University Press for National Bureau of Economic Research, 1961, Vol. I, Chap. 6.

[2] Geoffrey H. Moore, *Statistical Indicators of Cyclical Revivals and Recessions,* Occasional Paper 31, New York, NBER, 1950. Reprinted in *Business Cycle Indicators,* Vol. I, Chap. 7.

[3] *Business Cycle Indicators,* Vol. I. Chap. 3, "Leading and Confirming Indicators of General Business Changes."

[4] Julius Shiskin, *Signals of Recession and Recovery,* Occasional Paper 77, New York, NBER, 1961.

leading series, 15 roughly coincident, and 7 lagging, while 28 are termed "other U.S. series with business cycle significance." In addition, 7 series pertaining to industrial production in countries having important trade relations with the United States have been included.

Several considerations prompted the adoption of this large list. One was that it made it possible to provide a subclassification by economic processes. Thus, the roughly coincident series were divided into four groups: employment and unemployment, production, income and trade, and wholesale prices. The added series provided useful supplementary information about the types of economic process covered by the shorter list. Since up-to-date information was critical, in view of the uses to which the data would be put, indicators that were less adequate in some respects but available more promptly were included. For example, the ratio of wholesale prices to unit labor costs, which provides a rough indication of movements of profit margins in manufacturing and is available promptly on a monthly basis, supplements the quarterly series on profit margins and total profits, which do not appear until the second or third month after the end of the quarter to which they refer. Furthermore, it was believed that with the wider use of the indicators that would come with publication in a governmental report, there would be less likelihood of misinterpretation if judgments were based upon a broader view of the economy than is possible with a small number of series. Since it had always been recognized that leading, coincident, and lagging indicators by themselves comprise an incomplete basis for current business analysis, series representing other economic processes having an important bearing on business conditions in the United States were added. Most of these are factors, such as government expenditures or merchandise exports, that have significant influences on short-term economic fluctuations but have not behaved in a manner sufficiently consistent during business cycles to be readily classified as leading, coincident, or lagging.

Business Cycle Developments was published with the understanding that the list of leading, coincident, and lagging indicators would be selected by the National Bureau. Although some changes in the content of the publication have been made from time to time, with the advice and aid of an advisory committee appointed by the American Economic Association, these changes have been strictly limited in scope. With the passage of time the desirability of another comprehensive and systematic review of the list of indicators became apparent, and that is the purpose of this report. Periodic revisions are required because of the appearance of new economic time series, new findings of business cycle research, and the changing structure of the American economy.

The series that have been included on the lists are cyclical indicators in the broad sense. They are intended to be helpful in anticipating, measuring, and interpreting short-run changes in aggregate economic activity—that is, the complex of activities represented by such concepts as total production, employment, income, consumption, trade, and the flow of funds. Although the indicators have been selected largely with reference to their behavior during periods marked off by a simple chronology of cyclical peaks and troughs in aggregate economic activity (see Appendix F), their uses are by no means restricted to the identification of turning points from expansion to recession and from recession to recovery. The economic relationships and properties embodied in the set of indicators can be turned to account in analyses of various aspects of short-term economic developments, including the timing and magnitude of movements of particular economic aggregates such as the gross national product or nonagricultural employment, acceleration or retardation in growth, inflation or deflation, economic fluctuations in an industry or region, and so on. The merits and limitations of the indicators for such applications, however, are specific to the particular case, and are not necessarily closely related to those to which attention is given in this report. For example, experience has shown that the properties of the same list of indicators, for another country or for a state within the United States, can be expected to be broadly similar to those for the United States, but often there are differences in detail which need to be recognized to avoid misinterpretation.

SUMMARY

This paper presents the 1966 list of NBER cyclical indicators and a description of an explicit scoring plan that has been developed to help in the evaluation and selection of indicators. More than a hundred series have been evaluated, including those that came out well in previous studies and other series that appear promising for this purpose. This review is concerned chiefly with the series' quality as indicators of business expansions and contractions, and their classification and arrangement for effective use. It is limited to the role of economic time series as indicators of short-run movements in aggregate economic activity, and may not be relevant to their other uses.

The current study has extended the use of explicit criteria and objective standards employed by Mitchell, Burns, and Moore in establishing previous lists. This has been accomplished by a plan for assigning scores to each series within a range of 0 to 100. The scoring of each series, admittedly arbitrary in many respects, reflects our desire not only to make as explicit as possible the criteria for selecting indicators but also to increase the amount of information available to the user to aid in evaluating their current behavior.

The scoring plan includes six major elements: (1) economic significance, (2) statistical adequacy, (3) historical conformity to business cycles, (4) cyclical timing record, (5) smoothness, and (6) promptness of publication. When the subheads under most of these elements are counted, some twenty different properties of series are rated in all. This list of properties provides a view of the many different considerations relevant to an appraisal of the value of a statistical series for current business cycle analysis.

A high score for economic significance is accorded a series that measures a process with an important role in the analysis or forecasting of business cycle movements. In this connection, a series that broadly represents a strategic process is rated higher than one more narrowly defined, not only because the significance of the former for business cycle analysis is likely to be greater but also because its significance is less likely to shift as a result of technological developments, changing consumer tastes, and similar factors.

Statistical adequacy reflects the requirement that a series continue to measure the same economic process during future business cycle fluctuations, when the selected indicators are put to the hard test of current usage. Eight different elements are considered: type of reporting system, coverage of process, coverage of time unit, measure of revisions, measure of error, availability of descriptive material, length of period covered, and comparability throughout the period.

Consistent conformity of an indicator to past business cycles and consistent timing of its turning points relative to those in general business are obviously essential qualities in an indicator. A probability test is used to judge the statistical significance of these measures. In both cases, the recent record is given more weight than the earlier.

Since the beginning of a new cyclical phase can be discerned more promptly in a series which is smooth than in one which is irregular, smooth series are given higher ratings. Finally, for a series to be useful in current analysis, it must be up to date. Series that are released promptly, therefore, are assigned higher scores than those that lag in publication.

The assigned scores must be considered rough rather than precise measures of the relative usefulness of different series in analyzing short-term business conditions and prospects. Moreover, the scoring plan contains information not revealed by the over-all score alone. Since the scores assigned each of the factors considered indicate particular merits and limitations of series, the detailed results may be of assistance to both producers and users of economic data.

In classifying indicators into groups useful for purposes of business cycle analysis, it is desirable to take account of both their economic interrelationships and their cyclical behavior. The following scheme, designed to accomplish this, reflects the many necessary compromises among the purposes that a classification and presentation of indicators may serve, the varied interests and sophistication of users, and the simple as well as the intricate cyclical relationships among economic series.

1. The major principle of classification is a fourfold grouping by cyclical timing: leading, roughly coincident, and lagging indicators, and other selected series. The first three categories take into account timing at both peaks and troughs, but information is provided to distinguish timing at peaks from timing at troughs, since often there are significant differences. The fourth group includes economic activities that have an important role in business cycles but have displayed a less regular relation to them.

The new list of indicators includes 36 leading series, 25 roughly coincident, 11 lagging, and 16 unclassified by timing, or 88 in all; 72 are monthly and 16 are quarterly. This list includes 13 series not on the present National Bureau list, and omits 5 series. In addition, 14 series previously unclassified by timing are assigned a timing classification.

2. The type of economic process represented by the series is used as a secondary principle of classification, with emphasis on the processes that are important for business cycle analysis. The 88 U.S. series are classified into eight major groups: (1) employment and unemployment [14 series]; (2) production, income, consumption, and trade [8 series]; (3) fixed capital investment [14 series]; (4) inventories and inventory investment [9 series]; (5) prices, costs, and profits [11 series]; (6) money and credit [17 series]; (7) foreign trade and payments [6 series]; (8) federal government activity [9 series]. A ninth group, economic activity in other countries [7 series], is also provided. Each of these major categories is subdivided into economic processes that exhibit rather distinct differences in cyclical behavior. For example, under fixed capital investment, new investment commitments are distinguished from investment expenditures.

3. A short list of 25 series, drawn from the full list, is also presented. This more selective list includes 12 leading, 7 roughly coincident, and 6 lagging series; 21 are monthly and 4 quarterly. All these series have high scores and involve little duplication.

Thirty-four series included in the review are omitted from these lists. Some series with high scores are excluded because they do not seem to contribute sufficiently to warrant displacing others or increasing the length of the list. Some have relatively low scores, indicating that they have important limitations as cyclical indicators, however useful they may be in other respects.

Various composite indexes computed on the basis of the 1966 list are very similar to those based on the 1960 list. The principal contribution of the 1966 list, therefore, is the added information provided by new series and the new classification, especially in facilitating judgments on the performance of the several economic processes represented.

A broad summary of the classifications used for the indicators appears in Table 1: the timing classes, the major economic processes, and the minor economic groups within each timing and major process class. Some information on the characteristic leads or lags of the series in the minor economic groups is also provided. The reader will find this classification system more meaningful as he proceeds through this study, and he may also find Table 1 a convenient reference to help him follow the discussion.

TABLE 1
Cross-Classification of 88 Business Cycle Indicators by Cyclical Timing and Economic Process

Major Economic Group	Leading Indicators: Minor Economic Group	Leading Indicators: Series on Short List
1. Employment and unemployment	*Marginal employment adjustments* 5 series; 80% L; –5 mos.	Average workweek, manufacturing Nonagricultural placements
2. Production, income, consumption, and trade		
3. Fixed capital investment	*Formation of business enterprises* 2 series; 68% L; –6 mos.	Index of net business formation
	New investment commitments 8 series; 74% L; –6 mos.	New orders, durable goods Contracts and orders, plant and equipment Housing permits
4. Inventories and inventory investment	*Inventory investment and purchasing* 7 series; 80% L; –6 mos.	Change in manufacturing and trade inventories
5. Prices, costs, and profits	*Sensitive commodity price indexes* 1 series; 62% L; –2 mos.	Industrial materials prices
	Stock price indexes 1 series, 75% L; –4 mos.	Stock prices
	Profits and profit margins 4 series; 77% L; –5 mos.	Corporate profits after taxes Price/unit labor cost
6. Money and credit	*Flows of money and credit* 6 series; 79% L; –9 mos.	Change in consumer instalment debt
	Credit difficulties 2 series; 73% L; –5 mos.	
7. Foreign trade and payments		
8. Federal government activities		
All series	36 series; 76% L; –6 mos.	12 series; 75% L; –6 mos.

TABLE 1 (*Continued*)

Major Economic Group	Roughly Coincident Indicators	
	Minor Economic Group	Series on Short List
1. Employment and unemployment	*Job vacancies* 2 series; 62% C; 0 mos.	
	Comprehensive employment series 3 series; 79% C; −1 mo.	Employees in nonagricultural establishments
	Comprehensive unemployment series 3 series; 60% C; 0 mos.	Unemployment rate, total (inv.)
2. Production, income, consumption, and trade	*Comprehensive production series* 3 series; 63% C; 0 mos.	GNP in constant dollars Industrial production
	Comprehensive income series 2 series; 73% C; 0 mos.	Personal income
	Comprehensive consumption and trade series 3 series; 42% C; 0 mos.	Manufacturing and trade sales Retail sales
3. Fixed capital investment	*Backlog of investment commitments* 2 series; 38% C; 0 mos.	
4. Inventories and inventory investment		
5. Prices, costs, and profits	*Comprehensive wholesale price indexes* 2 series; 35% C; 0 mos.	
6. Money and credit	*Money market interest rates* 4 series; 44% C; 0 mos.	
	Bank reserves 1 series; 43% C; −1 mo.	
7. Foreign trade and payments		
8. Federal government activities		
All series	25 series; 53% C; 0 mos.	7 series; 59% C; 0 mos.

TABLE 1 (*Concluded*)

	Lagging Indicators		Other Selected Series
Major Economic Group	Minor Economic Group	Series on Short List	Minor Economic Group
1. Employment and unemployment	*Long-duration unemployment* 1 series; 75% Lg; +2 mos.	Unemployment rate, 15+ weeks (inv.)	
2. Production, income, consumption, and trade			
3. Fixed capital investment	*Investment expenditures* 2 series; 68% Lg; +2 mos.	Business expenditures, new plant and equipment	
4. Inventories and inventory investment	*Inventories* 2 series; 81% Lg; +4 mos.	Manufacturing and trade inventories	
5. Prices, costs, and profits	*Unit labor costs* 2 series; 72% Lg; +8 mos.	Labor cost per unit of output, manufacturing	*Comprehensive retail price indexes* 1 series
6. Money and credit	*Outstanding debt* 2 series; 62% Lg; +3 mos.	Commercial and industrial loans outstanding	
	Interest rates on business loans and mortgages 2 series; 72% Lg; +4 mos.	Bank rates on business loans	
7. Foreign trade and payments			Foreign trade and payments 6 series
8. Federal government activities			Federal government activities 9 series
All series	11 series; 71% Lg; +4 mos.	6 series; 68% Lg; +2 mos.	16 series

Note: The first figure below each minor economic group is the number of series in that group; the second figure is the number of leads (L), rough coincidences (C), or lags (Lg) as a percentage of the number of business cycle peaks and troughs covered by the series; the third is the median number of months that the series in the group lead (−) or lag (+) business cycle turns. See Table 6.

II

An Explicit Scoring System for Business Cycle Indicators

1. CRITERIA APPROPRIATE FOR SELECTING INDICATORS

In this review an attempt has been made to develop and apply a reasonably complete and explicit scoring system to aid in the selection and classification of indicators. Such a scoring system can be helpful in systematizing and testing professional judgments in selecting indicators, especially when the judgments are made by different investigators or by the same investigator at different times. It is also helpful in appraising the performance of different series in different types of situations. For example, has the behavior of a given indicator been similar or different at revivals as compared with recessions? Are the indicators which usually have long leads as reliable in other respects as those which usually have short leads? An explicit scoring system can also be used to help select series for various types of composite indexes or other special purposes. Finally, and perhaps most important, the information about each series that is provided by a scoring plan can help the analyst interpret the series' current performance in the light of its past behavior.

The objective of a scoring system for business cycle indicators is limited to evaluating their performance in relation to business cycles, and especially their usefulness in short-term forecasting. It is not concerned with other uses of the series, such as in studies of long-term growth or in governmental administration.

In their 1938 report on business cycle indicators, Mitchell and Burns specified the following characteristics for an ideal indicator of cyclical revivals and recessions.

1. It would cover half a century or longer, thus showing its relation to business cycles under a variety of conditions.
2. It would lead the month around which cyclical revival centers by an invariable interval—say three months, or better, six months. It would also lead the central month of every cyclical recession by an invariable interval, which might differ from the lead at revival.
3. It would show no erratic movements; that is, it would sweep smoothly up from each cyclical trough to the next cyclical peak and then sweep smoothly down to the next trough, so that every change in its direction would herald the coming of a revival or recession in general business.
4. The cyclical movements would be pronounced enough to be readily recognized, and give some indication of the relative amplitude of the coming change.
5. It would be so related to general business activity as to establish as much confidence as the nature of such things allows that its future behavior in regard to business cycles will be like its past behavior.[1]

Mitchell and Burns also noted the importance of having up-to-date figures, good seasonal adjustments, and detailed records of the indicator, its components, and related series.

These criteria were followed in selecting the 1938, 1950, and 1960 lists of indicators, various quantitative measures being devised to implement their application. In the present study we have divided the criteria into six broad types: (1) economic significance in relation to business cycles, (2) statistical adequacy, (3) conformity to historical business cycles, (4) consistency of timing during business cycles, (5) smoothness, and (6) currency.

Each type appears to have an essential role in a system for judging indicators. Economic significance implies that the behavior of a

[1] *Business Cycle Indicators,* Vol. I, pp. 165–166.

particular activity is both well understood and important in the theory of business cycles, i.e., an indicator's performance has a rational explanation. This provides some assurance that it will perform in the future about as well as in the past. On the other hand, unless the historical record of conformity and timing supports this theoretical role, the indicator's claim to a high rating is rendered doubtful; indeed, one might question any key role assigned to it in a business cycle theory.

Statistical adequacy ensures that a series will continue to measure the economic process it is intended to represent equally well during future business cycle fluctuations. In this sense it is an adjunct to the theoretical and historical requirements.

In current business cycle analysis a smooth series is more useful than an irregular one, because in the former a change in direction is more likely to denote the beginning of a new cyclical phase. In an irregular series a new trend must generally run for several months before one can be assured that a new cyclical phase has begun. Irregular series can be smoothed by various statistical devices, but these often impart biases of one sort or another and usually involve a loss of currency. In this sense smoothness and currency are related.

A series must, of course, be available promptly if it is to serve as a useful current indicator. A series which met all the other criteria well, but did not become available until five or six months after the period covered, is apt to be of little use in deciding whether a business cycle turn is imminent or under way, in determining the particular sectors in the economy in which weakness lies, or in selecting the appropriate countercyclical actions to take.

The conversion of these general types of criteria to an explicit scoring system involves many thorny problems. How, for example, can economic significance be judged? It cannot be defined here in terms of relative importance in gross national product, because some large sectors of GNP, such as the service industries, do not have a proportionate role in generating or contributing to cyclical fluctuations, and many relevant aspects of economic activity, such as the functioning of the credit markets, are not recorded in the national product accounts. A more appropriate definition of economic significance in this context would be the role in the cyclical process of the particular activity represented by the series. But in the absence of general agreement on a theory of business cycles, or a working model that reproduces their essential features, is it really possible to discriminate among series on this basis? Again, with most statistical producers each making a case for the reliability of their series, how can the statistical adequacy of different indicators be scored? In racking up a score for historical performance, what weight should be given to the record of conformity to past business cycles as compared with the consistency of past leads or lags? How much should a series be penalized because the most recent month's data are not available when current economic conditions and prospects are being reviewed?

There is certain to be an arbitrary element in the answers given to such questions, especially when the answers are put in quantitative terms. To a large extent, the results will reflect the judgment of the analyst, so that in the end an explicit scoring system may only shift some of the judgmental elements from the final stage of the selection of indicators to an earlier stage, where these implications are less clear. Yet an explicit scoring system does have important merits. It forces the investigator to specify what are his judgments of various properties of each indicator, and it provides a better basis for other investigators to review his work, extend its application, and improve upon it. The detailed results of applying a scoring plan should be valuable in aiding one's understanding of the theory, historical behavior, and methodology underlying the final set of indicators. By pointing to specific deficiencies, the scoring process may, indeed, promote the further development and improvement of our economic intelligence system.

It may be of interest to note that each of our six criteria has a bearing on the selection of data to be used in an econometric forecasting model. Economic significance surely embraces the idea that the variable is appropriate to include in the equations of the model. Measures of conformity to business cycles help to identify variables that, say, have more to do with long-run growth than with short-run fluctuations in the economy. Lagged variables are a necessary complement to a forecasting model; hence consistent leads or lags are features to be sought. Statistical adequacy, smoothness, and prompt availability at the time the model is to generate a forecast are naturally consequential to the model builder. This is not to say, of course, that the properties we have attempted to weigh in selecting indicators would be weighed in the same way in constructing an econometric model. The results might be quite different. But the criteria are broadly relevant to both approaches, and it is difficult to think of any criterion that is relevant to one but not to the other.

The method of this investigation has been to convert the general criteria listed above into an explicit scoring system with weights assigned by the authors. A separate scoring plan is set up for each criterion, under which a perfect indicator would earn 100 points. The six scores are averaged to obtain a single composite score.

It is recognized that this approach cannot provide an automatic or mechanical method of selecting indicators. The indicators we have selected are not simply those with the top scores. We believe the scheme does provide some objective tests of the quality of different indicators from the standpoint of their value in forecasting, and hence it exercises some control upon the judgment of the investigators in making the final selections. It also puts into clearer perspective the characteristic behavior and limitations of each indicator, and this knowledge is of potential value in the forecasting process itself when the movements of a given indicator are being evaluated. Finally, it may suggest ways in which these or other indicators can be improved to make them more useful for the present purpose.

2. ECONOMIC PROCESSES OR INDIVIDUAL INDICATORS?

A question that arose at the beginning of this investigation was whether to score individual series or groups of series representing broadly defined economic processes. Handling groups of closely related series as a unit has the advantage of avoiding the uncertain and arbitrary elements characteristic of individual series, such as the period they cover or the effects of a few extreme values on measures of cyclical behavior. In the 1950 NBER study, measures of the behavior of individual series were obtained first, then closely related groups of series were evaluated, and finally individual indicators were selected to represent each group. Among other things, this procedure made it possible to select series that had only recently been constructed and had only a brief record, if they were clearly superior in coverage or other respects to closely related series that had a longer record.

In terms of our list of six criteria, a case can be made for a combination of both approaches. That is to say, broadly defined economic processes might be evaluated under some of the criteria and individual indicators under others.

Under the criterion of economic significance it would seem best to evaluate groups of series representing a general type of activity, because theories which purport to explain business cycle phenomena do not ordinarily refer to particular indicators, but rather to generalized economic processes. On the other hand, since methods of compilation vary from series to series and change from time to time, statistical adequacy, smoothness, and currency pertain more directly to individual series. The value of a particular series for analyzing short-term business trends and prospects depends importantly on these properties.

The problem of the timing and conformity criteria is more complex. Here there is some advantage in scoring groups, because of the light that one series throws upon the behavior of another. For example, the recorded average lead at business cycle peaks of the unemployment rate (inverted) for married males is 15 months. But, because this series begins only in 1954, the average is based on observations at only two peaks (one a lead of 19, the other of 11 months). Related series that are available for a much longer period, such as the total unemployment rate, suggest that the tendency to lead is genuine but that the typical lead is closer to 4 months than to 15. Hence the evidence supporting the conclusion that unemployment, even of married males alone, tends to rise prior to a business cycle peak is much stronger than the limited evidence supplied by that series itself. Nevertheless, the historical record of each series is difficult to disregard. Can the same weight be given to a series with a poor conformity record as to another with a good conformity record merely because they fall in the same economic group?

Another troublesome question is how to group series for this purpose. The 1950 indicator study used a classification designed by Mitchell for his work on business cycles.[2] This classification reflected Mitchell's extensive knowledge of business cycle theory and history, the distinctions he had observed in the cyclical behavior of different processes, and the statistical series that were then available to fill the classifications. Today, the advances in our knowledge, the changes in cyclical behavior that have occurred, and the new statistical series that have been constructed all point to the need for a new classification.

On balance, the problems involved in combining group scoring with individual series scoring appeared too great to make it worthwhile, and each series has been scored independently. However, in making a final selection of indicators it is clearly of great importance to take into account the evidence provided by closely related series, and we have attempted to follow this practice.

For this, as well as for other purposes, we have devised a simple economic process classification. We believe that the following nine types would be generally recognized as strategic processes in business cycles, although different economists would divide them differently, substitute or add some other items, and certainly weigh them differently in their thinking:

1. Employment and unemployment
2. Production, income, consumption, and trade
3. Fixed capital investment
4. Inventories and inventory investment
5. Prices, costs, and profits
6. Money and credit
7. Foreign trade and payments
8. Federal government activities
9. Economic activity in other countries

Many series in the first two groups are measures of aggregate economic activity and are used to describe the broad movements of the business cycle and to determine the dates when business expansions and contractions begin or end. These two and the next four groups also include factors which are credited by students of the business cycle with a causal role in the cyclical process, that is, in the cumulative processes of expansion and contraction and in the reversal from expansion to contraction and from contraction to expansion. The last three groups represent processes which are not generally considered responsible for cyclical fluctuations in the United States, but which nevertheless importantly affect their pattern, amplitude, and duration. Many of the groups, in particular groups 6 and 8, include factors that reflect the implementation of governmental policy with respect to recession, unemployment, inflation, or other features of business cycles.

[2] See *Business Cycle Indicators,* Vol. I, pp. 214–215.

3. ECONOMIC SIGNIFICANCE

Economic significance is an essential element in selecting—as well as in using—business cycle indicators. It is the *sine qua non.* No matter how excellent an indicator's historical performance or statistical basis, it cannot be given great weight in analyzing short-term economic developments unless it measures or represents an activity with a key role in the cyclical process. But economic significance in this sense is also a most difficult element to evaluate in quantitative, objective terms. We have tried and rejected several alternative plans, including an attempt to consider each series' role in various explanations of the business cycle. We have also considered the possibility of omitting this element entirely from the explicit scoring scheme. In the final analysis, all the series on our list are economically significant; otherwise they would not have been considered at all. The question is whether it is better to try to recognize different degrees of significance, rough as the results are apt to be, than to leave this element out of the scoring plan and implicitly equate all series in this respect. Our judgment is that explicit scores for economic significance will make a contribution to the scoring system, enhancing both its rationalization and its discriminating power. We recognize, however, that there may be wide disagreement on the particular plan used for scoring as well as on the individual scores assigned for this element.

In order to evaluate the economic significance of indicators for business cycle analysis, it seems necessary to take into account at least two factors. One is the role of a given economic process in theories or hypotheses that purport to explain how business cycles come about or how they may be modified or controlled. The other is the breadth of coverage of a particular series representing that process.

The eight (or nine) types of economic process listed above appear to include all the variables deemed significant in modern business cycle analysis. Some factors that in earlier times attracted attention, such as variations in the weather or in the frequency of sunspots, are not covered. But the list does provide for "real" as well as "monetary" factors, for consumption as well as investment, for inventory as well as fixed capital investment, for costs as well as prices, for resource utilization rates as well as profits, for governmental as well as private activity, for international as well as domestic developments.

The eight categories are, however, rather broad. We can get closer to a specification of economic variables that are represented by statistical series if we subdivide them. Table 2 presents such a subclassification (column 1), developed with an eye to the types of economic indicators that are available and have proven to be of analytical interest in business cycle studies. The subclassifications are not exhaustive; others might well be added should occasion warrant. Moreover, they are not mutually exclusive. Some series might be classified in more than one of the subcategories. Thus, prices of industrial materials represent costs as well as prices, and so do interest rates. Orders for durable goods pertain to investment in capital equipment, to consumer purchases of autos and other durables, and to the accumulation of inventories of steel and other materials.

Despite these limitations, the subcategories constitute a list of economic variables that are of strategic interest in business cycle analysis, forecasting, and policymaking. Some of the available economic indicators represent these variables in comprehensive fashion; others are confined to particular sectors, components, or aspects. In columns 2 and 3 of the table the 122 indicators reviewed in this study are classified according to whether, conceptually, they are "broad" or "narrow" in coverage. Those that purport to cover the entire economy, or the "cyclically sensitive" portion of it, or major fractions thereof (such as all corporate activity, or total consumption or invest-

TABLE 2
Classification of 122 Series According to Economic Process and Breadth of Coverage

Type of Economic Process (1)	Broad Series[a] (2)	Narrow Series[b] (3)
1. Employment and unemployment		
Marginal employment adjustments		Av. workweek, mfg.
	Nonagri. placements	Accession rate, mfg.
		New hires, mfg.
		Rehires, mfg.
	Temporary layoffs	Layoff rate, mfg.
	Initial claims, unempl. insur.	
Job vacancies	Nonagri. job openings	
	Help-wanted ads	Executive help-wanted ads
Employment	Nonagri. man-hours, employees	
	Nonagri. man-hours, with job	
	Nonagri. man-hours, at work	
	Nonagri. empl., estab. survey	
	Nonagri. empl., household survey	
	Nonagri. empl., commodities	Nonagri. empl., services[c]
Unemployment	Unempl. rate, total	Unempl. rate, under 5 wks.
		Unempl. rate, 5–14 wks.
		Unempl. rate, 15+ wks.
	Unempl. rate, insured	
	Unempl. rate, married males	
2. Production, income, consumption, and trade		
Production	GNP, current $, expend. est.	
	GNP, constant $, expend. est.	
	GNP, current $, income est.	
	GNP, constant $, income est.	
	Industrial production	Steel ingot production
		Pass. car production
Income	Personal income	Labor income in mining, mfg., and construction
Consumption and trade	Bank debits outside N.Y.C.	
	Final sales, current $	
	Final sales, constant $	
	Mfg. and trade sales	Mfrs.' sales
		Wholesalers' sales
		Truck tonnage hauled
	Retail sales	Cons. expend., dur. goods
3. Fixed capital investment		
Formation of business enterprises	Net business formation	
	New incorporations	
New investment commitments	New orders, dur. goods	New orders, mach. and equip.
		New orders, mach. tools
	Constr. contracts, total	Housing starts
		Building permits, housing
	Contracts and orders, plant and equipment	New cap. approp., mfg.
		Comm. and indus. contracts
Backlog of investment commitments		Unfilled orders, dur. goods
		Cap. approp. backlog, mfg.

TABLE 2 (*Continued*)

Type of Economic Process (1)	Broad Series[a] (2)	Narrow Series[b] (3)
Investment expenditures	Gross priv. dom. invest., total	
	Gross priv. dom. invest., bus. sec.	
	New pl. and equip. expend.	
	Mach. and equip. sales and bus. constr. expend.	Prod. dur. equip. sales
		Equipment production
		New constr. expend., bus.
4. Inventories and inventory investment		
Inventories	Mfg. and trade inventories	Mfrs.' inventories, total
		Mfrs.' inventories, fin. goods
Inventory investment and purchasing	Change, bus. inventories	
	Change, mfg. and trade invent.	Purch. mat., % reptg. higher inventories
		Change, purch. mat. inventories
		Buying policy, prod. mat.
		Vendor performance
		Change, unfilled orders, dur.
		Change, dept. store stocks on hand and on order
5. Prices, costs, and profits		
Sensitive commodity price indexes		Indus. mat. prices
Stock price indexes	Stock prices, 500 common stocks	
Wholesale price indexes	Wholesale prices, exc. farm products and foods	Wholesale prices, mfd. goods
Retail price indexes	Consumer price index	
Unit labor costs	Labor cost per $ of real corp. GNP	Labor cost per unit, mfg.
Profits and profit margins	Corp. profits, total	
	Profits to income orig., corp.	Profits to sales, mfg.
		Price to labor cost, mfg.
6. Money and credit		
Flows of money and credit	Change, money supply and time deposits	
	Change, money supply	
	Total private borrowing	Change, consumer instal. debt
		Change, bank loans to bus.
		Change, mortgage debt
		New nonfarm mortgages recorded
	Corp. gross savings	Stock offerings, mfg. corp.
		Stock sales, N.Y.S.E.
Outstanding debt		Cons. instal. debt outst.
		Comm. and indus. loans outst.
Bank reserves	Free reserves	
Money market interest rates		Treasury bill rate
		Corp. bond yields
		Treasury bond yields
		Municipal bond yields
Interest rates on business loans and mortgages		Bank rates on bus. loans
		Mortgage yields, residential
Credit difficulties	Liab. of bus. failures	No. of large bus. failures
		Delinq. rate, all instal. loans
		Delinq. rate, direct auto loans

TABLE 2 (*Concluded*)

Type of Economic Process (1)	Broad Series[a] (2)	Narrow Series[b] (3)
7. Foreign trade and payments	Balance of payments	
	Merchandise trade balance	
	Exports	Export orders, dur. goods
		Export orders, machinery
	Imports	
8. Federal government activities	Surplus or def., income and prod.	
	Cash surplus or deficit	
	Cash receipts	
	Cash payments	Defense purchases
		Defense oblig., total
		Defense oblig., procurement
		New orders, defense products
		Military contracts

Note: This classification does not take into account the *statistical* coverage of the series; i.e., what fraction of the population it purports to cover is actually reported. For full titles of series, see Appendix G.

[a] Economy-wide; nonagricultural; manufacturing and trade; total corporate; commodity, consumption, or investment aggregates.

[b] Manufacturing; other sectors or components narrower than those listed under note a.

[c] See text.

ment), are considered "broad."[3] Series that pertain to a single industry (e.g., manufacturing) or to minor components of the "broad" series are placed in the "narrow" group.[4]

One of the theoretical advantages of broad coverage is that it provides protection against substantial changes in cyclical behavior that may arise from such factors as technological developments, changing consumer tastes, or the rapid growth or decline of single products or industries. A broad economic indicator may continue to perform well, or at least in representative fashion, even though some of its components deteriorate in this respect. Thus, one would expect total retail sales to continue to be an important indicator, while department store sales alone might diminish in significance.

The table tells us something about the economic significance of the several indicators and their relationship to one another in terms of economic coverage. We have not attempted to distinguish degrees of significance among the economic categories in which the series are classified. Hence we haye given all series in the "broad" column the same score, namely 75. Similarly, all series in the "narrow" column are given a score of 50. The assignment of the same score to all series within a column means, of course, that some obvious differences in coverage are ignored.

The result of this process is that all of the indicators considered in this review get scores of either 75 or 50 for economic significance, depending upon their coverage.[5] This does not mean that any economic series whatever would be entitled to such a score. The indicators

[3] This does not imply that their coverage is broad from a statistical point of view. Some of the "broad" series are based on limited statistical samples. This aspect of coverage is considered in section 4, below.

[4] The classification of service industry employment poses a problem, since it is currently a larger component of nonagricultural employment than the "cyclically sensitive" commodity-producing employment. Since the commodity sector could, while the service sector could not, be considered representative of employment from the cyclical point of view, the service series is relegated to the "narrow" group.

[5] The levels 75 and 50, while arbitrary, yield an average score for economic significance roughly similar to that for the other five categories in the scoring plan.

under review are already a highly selected group. Within it, it did not seem feasible or especially useful to make fine distinctions with respect to their significance for cyclical analysis and forecasting, apart from their breadth of coverage.

4. STATISTICAL ADEQUACY

A sound statistical method of compilation is a necessary condition for a good indicator, since it provides some assurance that the figures can be relied upon, in the future as in the past. Some of the considerations involved apply chiefly to the series as currently issued; others to the historical data.

An important requirement is that the series be based upon a reporting system. The aggregate it reflects should be obtained by summing reports on their activities made by respondents. Thus retail sales should be obtained by summing reports from retailers or consumers, manufacturers' orders by summing reports from manufacturers or buyers, employment by summing reports from employers or members of the labor force. This requirement may seem obvious, but some important series, such as the index of industrial production, or the index of net business formation, or even gross national product, are based largely upon indirect sources.

Good coverage is a second requirement. With careful collection, editing, and processing of returns, complete coverage is obviously best. But complete and accurate coverage is often difficult, partly because of its cost and partly because of the unwillingness of some respondents to report. When a sample is necessary, it should be a probability sample, for then a measure of the error that arises in estimating the universe from partial coverage can be provided. Other kinds of samples may also give good results, but they have the disadvantage that their accuracy cannot be expressed in quantitative terms. The mere size of the sample is not a sufficient criterion, for it is sometimes possible to obtain a more accurate series from a smaller sample than from a larger one. When reporting is poor and processing costs large, more careful handling of a smaller number of returns may result in a reduction of the reporting and processing errors that is greater than the error introduced by the smaller sample.

A statistic should cover the full period it represents; for example, a series representing a monthly total should cover the full month. For reasons of economy, some series refer to only one week or even one day of the month. This is a different kind of sample and, like other kinds, leaves something to be desired, especially when the figures are not accompanied by a measure of the error resulting from this short cut.

It is customary to release current statistics before all the returns are in. These "preliminary" figures are later revised at various intervals when more complete information becomes available. Thus, a substantial proportion of the returns in the sample of manufacturers from whom sales and orders data are collected become available by the twentieth of the month following that covered by the data, but the sample is more complete by the end of the month, and some returns come in during the following month. More nearly complete estimates for all manufacturing are available in the *Annual Survey of Manufactures,* while full detail for various products may become available only once every five years in a census of manufactures. The accumulation of better information leads to revisions.

Methods of seasonal adjustment also lead to revisions. For example, the moving average methods commonly used require more years of data to estimate seasonal factors for the current year than are available at the time the estimates for the current year are made. When the additional data do become available, the seasonal factors and the seasonally adjusted data are revised. It is clear that a measure of the extent and significance of seasonal and other revisions is a desirable supplement to a statistical series.[6]

A measure of the total error, from all sources, to which each figure is subject is therefore an important requirement for a sound statistical series. For business cycle studies, errors of the estimates of change are frequently more important than errors of the estimates of level. Apart from sampling errors, respondents make errors in reporting, statistical agencies make errors in processing or estimating, and compositors make errors in printing. Partly for theoretical reasons and partly because of costs, it is difficult to derive a measure of the total error. None of the statistical series covered in our review now provides such a measure, though efforts to obtain them in the survey of unemployment and related series are under way. The existence of closely related series often provides important clues to the errors to which any one of them is subject.

The factors discussed above apply to the currently issued data. But to appraise the usefulness of a series as a cyclical indicator, a historical record must also be available. From this point of view, two considerations are relevant: the period for which the series is available and the comparability of the series over time. A series going back many years obviously provides more information on its cyclical behavior than a short series. The producers of statistical series are often confronted with the dilemma of improving a series or maintaining its historical comparability. Both are important. Improvement is often necessary to reflect the forces which the series is designed to measure, to expand coverage, or to catch up with changes in the structure of the economy. However, breaks in comparability reduce the value of the series for historical analysis.

Finally, a full account of the survey methods (content of survey form, collection procedure, sampling, editing, coding, and other processing), the coverage both in terms of the respondents and the period, and the seasonal and related adjustment methods is an essential requirement for statistical series. On the other hand, although seasonal, trading-day, and smoothing adjustments contribute to the usefulness of statistical series in their role as business cycle indicators, electronic computers have made such auxiliary data available for all the business indicators considered in this review. For this reason, it seems unnecessary to score these factors.

5. CONFORMITY

A principal factor in judging the historical performance of indicators is their conformity to past business cycles. The National Bureau's index of conformity provides a simple measure of how faithfully each series has followed the business cycle chronology. A series that has

[6] When are preliminary statistics sufficiently accurate to be useful in interpreting short-term business trends and prospects? One approach to this question is to compare the magnitude of revisions with the magnitude of changes in the underlying trend. Thus, preliminary estimates of month-to-month changes might be considered acceptable if the subsequent revisions are on average smaller than the average month-to-month change in the underlying trend. The following formula expresses this criterion:

$$\frac{\bar{R}}{\bar{\bar{C}}} < 1,$$

where $\bar{R}$ is the average revision of the month-to-month changes and $\bar{\bar{C}}$ is the average month-to-month change in the trend-cycle component of the final series, both averages being taken without regard to sign.

Other ways of appraising the usefulness of preliminary figures are to determine whether revisions affect the direction of the month-to-month changes in the MCD curves or whether they substantially alter the proportion of "significant" month-to-month changes. For the derivation of $\bar{\bar{C}}$ and the MCD curves, see Julius Shiskin, *Electronic Computers and Business Indicators,* Occasional Paper 57, New York, NBER, 1957.

An extensive study of revisions of gross national product and its components is being carried out by Rosanne Cole as part of the National Bureau's study of short-term forecasting.

risen during every business expansion and declined during every contraction will have an index of +100; a series which has declined during every expansion and risen during every contraction will have an index of —100. Systematic leads and lags are taken into account. For example, if a series typically leads, an allowance is made for the average (median) lead in computing the conformity index. The conformity index is a type of correlation coefficient between the cyclical fluctuations in each series and those in aggregate economic activity. The business cycle chronology used in this study is recorded in Appendix F.

The length of the record upon which the conformity index is based, i.e., its statistical significance, needs to be taken into account. Following a scheme used in the 1950 NBER study, we have computed the probability, for a series covering a specified number of cycles, that the conformity index would reach the observed level. This probability, rather than the conformity index itself, is used in the scoring plan.

The conformity index, however, misses several important aspects of conformity. First, it is unaffected by extra cycles. For example, during the business cycle expansion of 1949–53, the extra declines in many series during 1951 are disregarded in computing conformity indexes, since only the change between levels at business cycle troughs and at business cycle peaks are considered. In analyses of current business cycle developments such extra movements may be misleading, as when a current decline in a series is interpreted as a signal of recession but eventually proves to be an extra cyclical phase having no general significance. Second, the conformity index does not distinguish early lapses in conformity from recent lapses. Yet recent lapses are a matter of greater concern than those which occurred many years ago, because of the ever-changing forces that shape the business cycle. Third, the conformity index does not take the amplitude of the cycle into account. A series which reveals a cycle clearly and decisively is more useful, other things equal, than one whose cyclical movements are mild and difficult to distinguish from other types of fluctuation.

Hence in our scoring plan the conformity index and its probability are supplemented by measures of extra cycles, recent lapses, and amplitude. It would be desirable, also, to take account of the relation between the amplitude of the movements in an indicator, particularly in the early months of a recession or recovery, and the amplitude of the business cycle, but that has not been done in the present study.[7]

6. TIMING

One of the most firmly established findings of business cycle research is that the cyclical movements in many different economic activities typically occur at somewhat different times; that is, some series lead and others lag. These relationships are of vital significance to the forecaster. Their nature and stability must therefore be recognized in a scoring system.

Several important aspects of timing are considered: the consistency with which timing comparisons of the same type (leads, rough coincidences, or lags) occur at successive business cycle turns;[8] the variability in length of (say) the lead, as measured by the dispersion about the average; the recency of defections from characteristic behavior; the presence of long-run shifts in timing; and the difference between timing at business cycle peaks and at troughs.

[7] Measures of this type were in a 1958 NBER report, *Measuring Recessions* (reprinted in *Business Cycle Indicators,* Vol. I, Chap. 5, pp. 120–161).

[8] Leads and lags are measured (in months) by comparing the date of the cyclical peak (or trough) in the series with the monthly business cycle peak (or trough) date, according to rules established for matching these turns. Leads (lags) are timing comparisons in which the cyclical turn in the series precedes (follows) the business cycle turn by one month or more. Rough coincidences overlap these, being defined as leads or lags of three months or less, including exact coincidences.

As in the case of conformity, a probability scheme for judging consistency of timing, developed in the 1950 study, is used here. It involves calculating the probability that as large a proportion of leads (or rough coincidences or lags) as that observed during the business cycle turns covered by the series could occur by chance. This allows for the fact that a given proportion of leads is more significant the larger the number of cycles covered. It takes account also of the possibility that the series may skip a particular cycle and hence fail to produce any timing comparison. Errors of the opposite kind, i.e., *extra* cycles, are allowed for under conformity, as noted above.

The length of the average lead or lag is of obvious importance in using indicators. It is difficult, however, to designate an ideal lead time. It might be argued, for example, that a lead of thirty months is too long to be useful in planning policies to combat inflation or recession, while a lead of three months does not provide enough time to muster the forces necessary for an effective attack. However, much depends on the variability about the average and the availability of other information. No one indicator should be considered in isolation, but rather as one among many factors in a developing situation. Let us suppose that one indicator leads by twenty-four months, another by twelve, and a third by six. Then early-warning signals of the end of expansion (contraction) could be observed as they unfold, and countercyclical policies systematically prepared. Furthermore, a series that lags regularly can also be helpful. It may confirm the doubtful signals of other series, or it may reveal developments that will eventually set the stage for a reversal of the cyclical tides.

In the light of these considerations, it does not seem possible to prefer one average lead time to another,[9] and we have, therefore, not assigned scores on the basis of these averages. However, the average (median) lead or lag is used to classify the indicators. That is, subject to qualifications noted below, an indicator is classed as leading if the median of all the timing comparisons is a lead of two months or more *and* if the number of leads, considered in relation to the number of business cycle turns covered by the series, is sufficient to reach an "acceptable" level on the probability scale mentioned above. Similarly, a series is classed as lagging if its median timing is a lag of 2 months or more and the number of lags is significantly large. A series is roughly coincident if it fails to satisfy the above criteria but exhibits a significant number of rough coincidences (timing observations that lie within a range of ± 3 months). Hence most roughly coincident series have median timing of -1, 0, or $+1$ months, though medians of ± 2 are possible (i.e., if with a median of ± 2 the series fails the probability test for leads or lags but qualifies for rough coincidences). The same significance level is used for all three classifications.[10]

[9] There is one rather exceptional situation that affords a basis for preference. In a few series with very long average leads, some of the individual leads approximate or even exceed the length of the corresponding business cycle phase. For example, the rate of change in the money supply reached its trough in December 1959, some fourteen months before the business cycle trough of February 1961, with which it is matched. Here the upturn in money even preceded the downturn in business (May 1960), and the series rose throughout the contraction. Such leads may, if they occur frequently, raise the question whether the series is positively or inversely related to business cycles. In any case, they make for difficulties in interpretation. For this reason, an unusually long average lead may be disadvantageous, other things equal.

[10] This is the same significance test used in the 1950 study, which was based upon a tabulation of the leads and lags of some 404 series with "acceptable" conformity. Cf. *Business Cycle Indicators,* Vol. I, p. 209. The record covered business cycles between 1854 and 1938. A similarly comprehensive record that includes the period since 1938 has not been compiled, but a tabulation limited to a group of 90 selected indicators for the period through 1961 gave results quite similar to the earlier one, considering the greater selectivity of the sample.

7. CURRENCY AND SMOOTHNESS

Prompt availability is an essential requirement of an indicator. In the counsels of practical men, a series that is current commands attention, whereas one that is out of date is apt to be disregarded. Thus, if a figure on corporate profits, surely a dynamic factor in business cycles, does not appear promptly after the quarter covered, it may not even be posted on a score sheet of current developments. On the other hand, more promptly available indicators, such as retail sales and unemployment, will get heavy weight in the decision-making process. It is unfortunately the case that judgments of the current outlook are often based upon a poor representation of series because they must be made before reports for all the indicators are in.

The availability of daily figures (prices of industrial raw materials or of common stocks) or weekly figures (retail sales or initial claims for unemployment insurance) must be counted in favor of an indicator. Such data are often helpful in making an early estimate for the current month, and occasionally they are useful directly in determining a cyclical turning point. As a rule, the shorter the time unit in which data are reported, the shorter the lag in their availability to the analyst.

A smooth series has the advantage that it is more likely than an irregular one to give prompt notice of the beginning of a new cyclical phase. An ideal indicator would be one that changed direction only in the event of a recession or recovery. This explains in large part the efforts of economists and statisticians to disentangle the underlying cyclical movements of economic series from other types of change, especially seasonal and irregular fluctuations.

Economic series vary a great deal in their smoothness. None meets the ideal, though some come close to it. Indeed, many indicators that meet other criteria well are highly irregular, for example, housing starts or the liabilities of business failures. A study of 150 economic series showed that the month-to-month changes are on average "cyclically significant" in only about 25 per cent; even in these, not all of the month-to-month changes are cyclically significant.[11] Since irregularities dominate the short-term changes of the other series, comparisons over longer spans must usually be made to detect cyclical changes.

This points up the fact that higher degrees of smoothness can be achieved either by observing the series over longer intervals, e.g., comparing the latest month's figure with the figure six months ago, or by consolidating the figures into longer time units, as for example by a moving average. Either way there is a loss in timeliness, because recent changes in direction are obscured. Because of this relationship between smoothness and currency, both factors must be taken into account in evaluating indicators. For example, there is generally a net advantage in weekly over monthly data that are equivalent in other respects, even though weekly data are often much more erratic in their movements. The reason is that the weekly data can, if necessary, be converted to four- or five-week moving totals, in which case they will be as smooth as the corresponding monthly data, and as a rule more up to date. The advantage is even greater, of course, when the monthly data pertain to only one week in the month. Monthly data possess similar advantages over quarterly figures.

It should be noted that preliminary estimates for most series are usually more erratic than the final estimates. Revisions of seasonal

[11] "Cyclical significance" is defined as a condition in which the average change in the irregular component ($\bar{I}$) of a series is smaller than in the cyclical component ($\bar{C}$). The ratio, $\bar{I}/\bar{C}$, generally diminishes as the span over which change is measured increases. See *Business Cycle Indicators,* Vol. I, p. 607.

adjustments generally yield smoother adjusted data, and so do revisions that result from a larger reporting sample. Our measures of smoothness are based upon the historical record, not the current record. Eventually, we may be able to devise measures appropriate to current data. A justification for the present method is that for comparisons among series, historical smoothness is probably highly correlated with current smoothness.

Measures of smoothness, currency, and timing should, ideally, be considered in relation to one another. The loss of currency that occurs when an irregular series is smoothed may be offset, in some degree, by a long lead. Similarly, a series that is not promptly available but has a long lead may be as useful as a series that comes out promptly but has a shorter lead. For example, the gross accession rate for manufacturing is not available as promptly each month as the broader series, nonagricultural placements, and its irregular fluctuations are larger, but the accession rate nearly always has shown a longer lead. If the accession rate were smoothed by, say, a three-month moving average, its loss of currency on this account as well as its publication lag would still not quite offset the advantage of its longer lead.[12] This illustrates the desirability of evaluating the leads and lags of indicators after smoothing them to an equivalent degree and taking into account both their publication lag and the additional lag produced by smoothing. We have not been able to do this systematically in this study, but Appendix E shows the effect on the median lead or lag of the 72 leading, coincident, and lagging indicators of adjusting them to a roughly equivalent degree of smoothness by simple moving averages. In general, the effect on the sequences among the indicators is not great, though the leads of some highly erratic series are substantially reduced.

8. COVERAGE OF SERIES UNDER REVIEW

The present review has covered 122 series. Included are the 80 U.S. indicators presently published in *Business Cycle Developments* and some 42 additional series which have at one time or another been considered for inclusion. The additional series cover a wide range, but there is some emphasis on areas where the present list is relatively thin, such as financial indicators.

The "population" of series upon which the review is based, therefore, is by no means a random collection of economic data. This was equally true of the more extensive reviews made previously by the National Bureau. In all cases the series considered for review represented processes that were judged, in some degree, economically significant in the analysis of business cycles. In some instances, however, processes that might have been considered significant were omitted, or poorly represented, because adequate monthly or quarterly data are not available. The possibility remains that some important indicators have been overlooked. Suggestions to this effect would be welcomed by the authors.

[12] At the nine business cycle turns covered by both series, 1945–61, the accession rate led placements on all but one occasion (when they were coincident) and the median lead was 4 months. The $\bar{I}/\bar{C}$ ratios for the two series are, respectively, 3.20 and 1.23. Smoothing by a three-month moving average would reduce the former to about the level of the latter, namely, 1.11. Allowing for a one-month lag on account of the centering of the three-month average and another month for publication lag would cut the median effective lead of the accession rate relative to placements to 2 months, and it would have led placements at 5 turns, coincided twice, and lagged twice. Placements are analogous to the new-hires component of the accession rate, and this component often moves later than the accession rate—i.e., later than the other component, rehires. For a discussion of some of these relationships, see the report by Charlotte Boschan in the 44th Annual Report of the National Bureau, New York, 1964, pp. 106–110.

9. APPLICATION OF THE SCORING PLAN ILLUSTRATED

The way this scoring method was applied can be illustrated by the series, new orders received by durable goods manufacturers, an important leading indicator. It received the relatively high score of 78.

The scores assigned for each element considered in evaluating a series were posted on a special "scoresheet." Many of the entries were derived from detailed statistical records, posted on a "worksheet for timing, conformity, and smoothness." Most of these, in turn, were based upon the business cycle measures developed by the National Bureau of Economic Research and described in the volume *Measuring Business Cycles* by Burns and Mitchell. The scoresheet and worksheet for new orders of durable goods are shown here as Tables 3 and 4. This record covers the full period for which the series is available, 1920–65. For series that start before 1948, such as this one, a second scoresheet covering the period 1948 to 1965 is also prepared (not illustrated here), so that the scores for all series can be compared for a common, recent period, 1948–65. (See Appendix D.) The detailed instructions for scoring are given in Appendix A.

First, the series was assigned 75 for economic significance, the higher of the two levels adopted for this category. The strategic role of investment in capital goods in business cycles is generally recognized. This series records an early stage of the investment process, not only in the sense that it records orders of equipment largely for future delivery, but also in that it includes orders placed for materials to be used in the production of capital goods. The materials, such as steel and lumber, enter into structures as well as equipment, and the finished goods, such as automobiles, aircraft, and machinery, include those purchased by business enterprises, consumers, and government. Hence, directly and indirectly, it has very broad coverage, warranting its assignment to the "broad" rather than the "narrow" group.

With respect to the next item, statistical adequacy, the series is assigned the full 20 points for "reporting system" since it is compiled from reports sent to manufacturing companies for statistical purposes only. It accumulates another 15 points because it is based upon a probability sample, and 10 more because the data cover the full month, and not some portion of it.

The compiling agency has not yet published a measure of the magnitude of revisions or the sampling error for this series; hence, no points are assigned for these items. On the other hand, full credit (5 points) is given for the availability of a detailed description of the series.

In order to give some weight to the length of the historical period covered by a series, 2 points are assigned for each five years covered, up to 50 years. The earliest segment of the series on new orders for durables begins in 1920; hence it is counted as covering 45 years, and scores 18 points.

With respect to comparability over time, it is necessary to take account of the serious breaks in the series in 1928 and 1938. There is some doubt, also, about its comparability before and after 1953, because of improvements in compilation procedures, but we decided to consider it essentially continuous since 1948. The series therefore scores 4 points for comparability. For statistical adequacy as a whole, the series achieves a mark of 72 points ($20 + 15 + 10 + 5 + 18 + 4$).

The timing, conformity, and smoothness worksheet (Table 4) shows that new orders conformed to the business cycle in all the phases for which data are available—nine expansions and nine contractions. That is, it rose during every expansion and fell during every contraction, when allowance is made for the

TABLE 3
Sample Scoresheet for Indicators

RIES: Manufacturers' New Orders, Durable Goods Industries,

NBER, 1920-28; NICB, 1929-38; OBE, 1939-46; Census, 1947-65

BCD # 6 NBER # 6,84 & 6,91

	SCORE
I ECONOMIC SIGNIFICANCE (20%) (importance in business cycle theory, broadness of coverage in the economy)	75

I STATISTICAL ADEQUACY (20%)

Current data:		Historical data:	
1. Reporting system (based upon reports obtained directly from respondents, or administrative records such as tax reports, or similar sources)	20	7. Duration (time period covered)	18
2. Coverage of process (universe, probability sample or other types of sample)	15	8. Comparability of historical series Absence of breaks in comparability	0
3. Coverage of time unit (full calendar month or quarter; or selected week or day)	10	Last segment 15 yrs. or longer	4
4. Revisions (measure of frequency and magnitude)	0		
5. Measure of error (availability of, for total error or sampling error)	0		
6. Description (completeness of, for compilation or estimation methods)	5		

SCORE: 72

CONFORMITY (20%) (to the business cycle)

1. Conformity probability (that as large a number of movements in the series which conform to cyclical movements in general business could occur by chance)	60
2. Extra turns (absence of cyclical turns in the series that do not correspond with turns in general business)	12
3. Recent lapses (absence of lapses in conformity since 1948)	10
4. Amplitude (extent to which series undergoes clear cyclical movements)	6

SCORE: 88

TABLE 3 (*Concluded*)

		SCOR
IV TIMING (20%) (consistency with which timing comparisons of the same type--leads, rough coincidences, or lags--occur at successive business cycle turns)		
Peaks		
1. Timing class	Leads	
2. Probability (that as large a number of leads--or rough coincidences or lags--as that observed during the business cycle turns covered by the series could occur by chance)	55	
3. Dispersion (variability in the lengths of lead or lag)	0	
4. Recent lapses (recency of defections from typical behavior)	20	
		75
Troughs		
1. Timing class	Leads	
2. Probability	58[a]	
3. Dispersion	14	
4. Recent lapses	20[a]	
		92
Peaks and Troughs		84
V CURRENCY (10%)		
1. Promptness (interval after period covered that statistic becomes available)	80	
2. Daily or weekly reports (availability of daily, weekly, or 10-day reports)	0	80
VI SMOOTHNESS (10%) (estimate of the likelihood that a change in direction denotes the beginning of a new cyclical phase)		60
		AVERA SCOR
VII SUMMARY		
Peaks	based on leads at peaks and leads at troughs	76
Troughs		79
Peaks and Troughs		78

a Timing accepted for rough coincidences: probability score 7, lapses 0.

Note: Percentage figures in parentheses next to major headings show weights assigned in computing average scores. Scoresheet actually used did not include explanatory statements.

Sample Worksheet for Measures of Timing, Conformity, and Smoothness

Manufacturers' New Orders, Durable Goods Industries
NBER, 1920-28; NICB, 1929-38; OBE, 1939-46; Census, 1947-65

BCD # 6.
NBER # 6,84 & 6,91

Business Cycle Peak	June 1869	Oct. 1873	Mar. 1882	Mar. 1887	July 1890	Jan. 1893	Dec. 1895	June 1899	Sep. 1902	May 1907	Jan. 1910	Jan. 1913	Aug. 1918	Jan. 1920	May 1923	Oct. 1926	Aug. 1929	May 1937	Feb. 1945	Nov. 1948	July 1953	July 1957	May 1960
Lead(-)or Lag(+)at Peak(mos.)[1]															-4	-11		-5	-35	-3	-6	-19	-13
Expansion Conformity[2]															++	+	+	+	+	+	++	+	+
Business Cycle Trough	Dec. 1870	Mar. 1879	May 1885	Apr. 1888	May 1891	June 1894	June 1897	Dec. 1900	Aug. 1904	June 1908	Jan. 1912	Dec. 1914	Mar. 1919	July 1921	July 1924	Nov. 1927	Mar. 1933	June 1938	Oct. 1945	Oct. 1949	Aug. 1954	Apr. 1958	Feb. 1961
Lead(-)or Lag(+)at Trough(mos.)[1]														-6	-2		0	-2	-2	-4[c]	-11	-3	-1
Contraction Conformity[2]															-	-	-	-	-	-	-	-	-

	No. of Business Cycle Turns Covered	No. of Extra Specific Cycle Turns	Total No. of Comparisons Made	Number of: Leads, 4 Mos. or More	Leads, 1-3 Mos.	Coincidences, Exact	Coincidences, Rough[3]	Lags, 1-3 Mos.	Lags, 4 Mos. or More	Per Cent of Business Cycle Turns Covered: Leads	Coincidences, Exact	Coincidences, Rough[3]	Lags	Median Lead(-) or Lag(+) (months)	Mean Lead(-) or Lag(+) (months)	Standard Deviation of Leads & Lags (months)	Longest Lead (months)	Longest Lag (months)	Timing Probability	Timing Rejected or Accepted for
Peaks	10	1	8	7	1	0	1	0	0	80	0	10	0	-8 1/2	-12.0	10.1	-35	-3	.0202	Leads
Troughs	10	1	9	3	5	1	6	0	0	80	10	60	0	-2	-3.4	3.1	-11	0	.0079/.2207	Leads/R.C.
Peaks & Troughs	20	2	17	10	6	1	7	0	0	80	5	35	0	-4	-7.5	8.4	-35	0	.00034	Leads

Conformity				
	No. of Phases Covered	Index	Conformity Probability	Accepted or Rejected
Exp.	9	+100	.0020	Accepted
Con.	9	+100	.0020	Accepted
Full Cycle	18	+100	.0000038	Accepted

Specific Cycle Amplitude per Month	
Rise	+3.14
Fall	-2.45
Rise & Fall	2.80

Period Covered	$\overline{CI}$	$\overline{I}$	$\overline{C}$	$\overline{I}/\overline{C}$	MCD	$\overline{I}/\overline{C}$ for MCD Span	Average Duration of Run: CI	I	C	MCD
Jan.'53-Sept.'65	3.76	3.33	1.51	2.20	3	.66	1.81	1.58	8.44	4.41

[1] Timing comparisons are footnoted as follows if they apply:

[a] Equal to or longer than the corresponding business cycle phase.

[b] Comparison crosses an opposite specific cycle turn.

[c] Comparison rejects a competing specific cycle turn..

[2] A plus (+) signifies a rise and a minus (-) a decline during a business cycle expansion or contraction, taking into account the median lead or lag of the series.

[3] Includes leads of 1-3 months, exact coincidences, and lags of 1-3 months.

Notes: For definitions of timing, conformity, and amplitude measures, see Arthur F. Burns and Wesley C. Mitchell, Measuring Business Cycles, National Bureau of Economic Research, New York, 1949, Chapter 5. Note, however, that the conformity measures used here, which take leads or lags into account, are based on the median lead or lag of the series (in months) rather than the stages formerly used. For descriptions of the probability measures, see Geoffrey H. Moore, Statistical Indicators of Cyclical Revivals and Recessions, Occasional Paper 31, NBER, New York, 1950. For definitions of smoothness (MCD and $\overline{I}/\overline{C}$) and related measures, see Julius Shiskin, Electronic Computers and Business Indicators, Occasional Paper 57, NBER, New York, 1957. The last two references are reprinted in Business Cycle Indicators, Chapters 7 and 17, respectively.

average (median) lead of the series with respect to business cycles. The probability that such a result could have been obtained for a series that is randomly related to the business cycle is calculated to be .002 for expansions and contractions separately, and is still smaller for expansions and contractions combined. Our formula assigns the series the maximum number of points (60) for this measure of conformity. Since there were no lapses in conformity after 1948, an additional 10 points is scored here. However, the series had an extra cyclical turning point at peaks (January 1951) and an extra turning point at troughs (January 1952); hence it receives only 12 of the 20 possible points on this item. The average specific cycle amplitude per month is a moderately high 2.80 per cent, which yields 6 points out of a possible 10. Thus, for the various items grouped under conformity, new orders for durables total to 88 points (60 + 12 + 10 + 6).

Under timing, calculations are made for peaks and troughs separately and combined, on the basis of the entries on the worksheet. At peaks, this series led in all cases except 1929, where no timing comparison could be made; at troughs, leads also prevailed except for the coincident timing in 1933 and the absence of a timing comparison in 1927. The median timing was a lead of 8 months at peaks and 2 months at troughs. This record qualified the series as a leader at peaks and at troughs, with timing probability scores of 55 and 58 points respectively out of 60. Because of the high dispersion at peaks (standard deviation, 10.1 months), it failed to receive any points for this item. But, with a smaller dispersion at troughs (standard deviation, 3.1), it received 14 out of 20 possible points. Twenty additional points were credited because a timing comparison was made at every business cycle turn since 1948. Thus new orders for durables received 75 points for timing at peaks, 92 for timing at troughs, or an average of 84 for peaks and troughs combined.

This series is credited with 80 points for currency since an advance release comes out before the twentieth of each month, with data for the preceding month. There is no weekly estimate; therefore, no points could be added for this.

Several measures of smoothness are given on the worksheet.[13] The one used for scoring monthly series is the number of "months for cyclical dominance" (MCD), which for new orders is 3. Hence, our rules yield 60 points for smoothness.

Our rules assign equal weight to economic significance (75), statistical adequacy (72), conformity (88), and timing (84), and half weight to currency (80) and smoothness (60). The average for new orders for durables is therefore 78, which is the final score.

It must be emphasized that the absolute value of the scores for each criterion or for all combined has no significance. Its function is to aid in the relative evaluation of one series compared with another. In judging the scores for the individual series, therefore, it is important to consider their place in the frequency distribution of the scores for all the series covered by the study, and their relation to the average scores for the various items. These are given in Table 5.

The frequency distributions show that no series received a final score as high as 90 and that only 4 scored 80 or better. The average score was 62. Fifty-seven received a score of 75 for economic significance. This is consistent with the fact that the sample of series included in this study was selected with a view to their broad economic significance. According to the scheme for judging the statistical adequacy of the series, it turned out that only 4 had a score of 80 or over and none over 90.

Twenty-two series received a score of 90 or more for conformity, but 15 series scored below 50. The record on this criterion is again related to the design of the sample, which was

[13] For a discussion of the meaning and uses of these measures, see *Business Cycle Indicators,* Vol. I, pp. 535–545, 604–609.

TABLE 5
Distribution of Scores for 120 Indicators

Score	Economic Significance	Statistical Adequacy	Conformity	Timing	Smoothness	Currency	Final Score
	(number of series)						
100	...	...	...	...	26	17	...
95–99	...	...	6	...	...	...	...
90–94	...	...	16	2	...	...	...
85–89	...	1	15	3	...	...	1
80–84	...	3	14	11	32	44	3
75–79	57	17	17	5	...	...	7
70–74	...	25	18	5	...	...	14
65–69	...	23	7	11	...	...	33
60–64	...	29	3	6	27	1	20
55–59	...	12	2	12	...	...	15
50–54	63	5	7	9	...	10	8
45–49	...	3	2	4	...	...	10
40–44	...	1	2	12	13	34	5
35–39	...	...	...	5	...	...	4
30–34	...	1	1	2	...	...	...
25–29	...	...	1	6	...	7	...
20–24	...	...	4	5	7	...	...
15–19	...	...	1	5	...	...	...
10–14	...	...	...	6	...	...	...
5–9	...	...	1	9	...	...	...
0–4	...	...	3	2	15	7	...
Total	120	120	120	120	120	120	120
Average score	62	66	72	48	62	61	62

Note: Based on scores for full period covered by series. Two series (export orders of durables and export orders of machinery) are omitted because complete set of measures is not available.

selected mainly with an eye to series that conform regularly to business cycles, but it included some strategic series that conform poorly.

The timing scores are not as high as the conformity scores. Only 2 series had a timing score of 90 or better for peaks and troughs combined, and nearly half had timing scores under 50. The reason for the wide distribution is the same as for conformity.

For currency, or promptness of publication, only 17 series received a perfect score. These are series which are available by the twentieth of the month following that covered by the data and for which weekly or daily figures are available. Twenty-six series met our highest standard for smoothness.

Of the various elements scored separately, the highest average was attained by conformity (72) and the lowest by timing (48). Since no adjustment for such differences was made before computing the average score for each series, the elements with the highest average scores implicitly received more weight. It is to be noted, however, that if conformity is averaged with timing to attain a single score for historical performance during business cycles, the differences among the factors is small: all average between 60 and 66.[14]

[14] As a partial test of the scoring plan, a cumulated random series (i.e., a series with random first differences) was constructed from a table of random numbers to provide monthly observations over a 45-year period. This artificial series was adjusted so that

10. INTERPRETATION OF SCORES

The assigned scores should be considered rough rather than precise measures of the relative usefulness of different series in analyzing short-term business conditions and prospects. Despite our attempt to provide an objective appraisal of economic time series, many arbitrary elements, where judgments could differ considerably, enter into the design and execution of the plan. This is particularly true of the assignment of weights for the various factors, such as economic significance or statistical adequacy. If other investigators prepared a similar scoring program, it would no doubt differ in many respects from ours. We would venture the guess, however, that there would be a fairly high correlation between their scores and ours.

The precise value of the final score, therefore, has limited significance. It is a convenient symbol of success, like the grades assigned to students on an examination. The results depend to a degree upon the questions asked, the points assigned to each, and the judgment of the examiner in evaluating the responses. But the scoring plan conveys other information, not revealed in the final score. The scheme sets forth the many different factors that need to be taken into account in appraising indicators. Altogether, 20 different items are rated for each series. While there can be disagreement about their relative importance, we believe there would be general agreement on their relevance. Furthermore, the scores assigned point to particular merits and limitations of series, and in this way may be of assistance to both producers and users of statistics. A detailed examination of them may suggest which series are worth improving and in what respects improvements are needed. Thus, series which have low ratings for promptness of publication, but high ratings for economic significance and historical record, might be worth speeding up. Series whose principal defect is a large erratic movement might be intensively studied to find the causes and possible cures for this defect. In any case, users of the statistics can be forewarned of their limitations, and qualify their interpretations accordingly.

---

the expected average month-to-month change without regard to sign was equal to 5 per cent. Its MCD proved to be 3, and its smoothness score was 60. Scores for conformity and timing were obtained on the assumption that the series began at four alternative hypothetical dates (January 1919, June 1919, January 1920, and June 1920). In all four cases, the conformity score was 0. In three cases the timing score was also 0, and in one it was 26. This indicates, as we would expect, that series with cyclical properties but basically unrelated to the U.S. business cycle are unlikely to achieve scores that approach those achieved by the economic indicators included in this study.

III

Problems of Classification and Presentation

The implementation of the scoring plan described above provides a large amount of data relevant to the classification, presentation, and interpretation of indicators. How should these data be used in reaching decisions on the most effective type of classification and presentation? Let us examine four of the principal problems involved.

1. DIFFERENCES IN TIMING AT PEAKS AND TROUGHS

The National Bureau's classification of indicators that is presently in use ignores differences between timing at peaks and timing at troughs. Thus series in the leading group are so classified because they usually lead at both peaks and troughs; the case is similar with series in the roughly coincident and lagging groups. The 1950 study of indicators revealed, and subsequent studies have confirmed, that a substantial proportion of the economic time series that conform well to business cycles and are fairly regular in their timing do exhibit similar timing at peaks and troughs. In the 1950 study, this proportion was about 60 per cent. Nevertheless, this leaves a fairly large number of series whose timing at peaks is different, in varying degree, from what it is at troughs.

It is clear that many of these differences are statistically valid and economically significant. For example, the unemployment rate has usually reached its cyclical low point and begun to rise prior to business cycle peaks, but has reached its high and turned down only after a business cycle recovery has begun. The average timing at peaks since the 1930's is a lead of 4 months, while the average at troughs is a lag of 2 months. The difference is statistically significant. Leads at peaks have occurred on 4 out of 6 occasions, and at troughs lags have occurred 5 times out of 7. The explanation appears to be that during the advanced stages of a business cycle expansion the labor force continues to rise at a more or less steady rate while employment rises at a decreasing rate, owing to various economic obstacles that impede expansion, such as higher costs or the difficulty of finding skilled personnel. Consequently the gap between the labor force and employment—that is, unemployment or, in relative form, the unemployment rate—starts to rise before employment (or output) starts to decline. At troughs in business activity, unemployment often continues to rise for a time because the continuing growth in the labor force is larger than the initial, usually modest, rise in employment. The recovery in employment is relatively slow partly because an increase in output at this stage can be achieved without a commensurate increase in labor input, and partly because an increase in labor input can be brought about more effectively by lengthening the workweek than by adding new workers.

An example of the opposite type of difference is provided by personal income, which has frequently lagged briefly at business cycle peaks and led by a month or two at troughs. Here the rising trend of relatively stable or even countercyclical types of income is apparently responsible. Shifts in occupational composition toward white-collar jobs have favored relatively stable types of income, and the growth of transfer payments such as unemployment benefits has contributed a stabilizing, countercyclical element. The net result of these and certain other changes has been to reduce the cyclical swings in total personal income relative to those in output, and to produce short lags at peaks and short leads at troughs.

If differences of this sort were recognized in the classification and arrangement of indicators, the result would be that one classification would apply to peaks and another to troughs. There would, of course, be substantial elements of similarity between the two, since many series behave in broadly similar fashion at both turns. But recognition of the differences would enhance the value of the classification for those who wish to make the best use of the information on timing and adapt it to the current economic situation. During expansions, when indicators are studied with a view to predicting a peak in the business cycle, or at least identifying it when it comes, it would be helpful to have a classification pertinent to peaks. Similarly, during recessions the most relevant classification would be one pertaining to troughs.

On the other hand, dual classification would be more difficult to justify because less statistical evidence would be available to judge each case and the problem of presentation might be complicated. Thus, even for a fairly long series such as personal income, only 8 timing observations are available at peaks and 9 at troughs. When secular shifts in timing have occurred, only the recent observations will be pertinent for a current classification, and for short series these are all that are available. Inconvenience and confusion might result from shifting from one classification during expansions to another during recessions. This would be particularly serious if an error in recognizing a business cycle turning point occurred.

2. DIFFERENCES IN LENGTH OF LEAD OR LAG

The three categories hitherto used to distinguish types of timing—namely, leading, roughly coincident, and lagging—do not distinguish differences in length of lead or lag, or at best do so crudely. The term roughly coincident has been used to denote leads or lags of three months or less, including exact coincidences. Hence this category overlaps the other two. It fits well those series that match business cycle turns closely, sometimes coinciding and sometimes leading or lagging by a month or two or three. But it produces an ambiguity with respect to series that, say, consistently lead by only two or three months. They might be considered either leading or roughly coincident. As noted earlier, personal income has generally led business upturns, mostly by one or two months. Does it lead at troughs or is it roughly coincident?

The problem is a general one, since leads or lags can be of various lengths, and the differences in length are often significant. The gross accession or hiring rate, for example, has generally led business cycle turns by a longer interval than has the average workweek, probably because the former pertains to a change in labor input, the latter to the level of input. In other words, the hiring rate can decline for a considerable time; but until it reaches the level of the separation rate, no decline in employment will occur. A drop in the workweek, on the other hand, has an immediate impact on labor input. Again, leads of many series at business cycle peaks have generally been longer, at least in the postwar period, than at troughs. That is to say, a typical lead at peaks has represented a longer span than at troughs. But if length of lead is not recognized in the classification, this difference may pass unnoticed.

The importance of differences in length of lead becomes even clearer when one takes account of the fact that often it makes good economic sense to turn a lagging indicator into a leading indicator by inverting it, and vice versa. That is, instead of observing that the downturn in, say, finished goods inventories lags behind the downturn in business, one can observe that the downturn in inventories leads the next upturn in business. The inventory decline can be a consequence of the business contraction that it follows, but it also can be a factor contributing to the ensuing business recovery, since the depletion of inventories produces conditions that may lead to an increase in output. Similar considerations apply to interest rates, unit-labor costs, the rate of change in the money supply, and many other series. Whether a series is a leading or lagging indicator, therefore, depends not merely on how it behaves but also on how one regards its role in the cyclical process, and especially on whether causes or effects are being considered.

Decisions with respect to whether timing comparisons should be made on a positive or inverted basis have a bearing on the question whether to classify indicators according to length of lead, because a series with consistently short lags on a positive basis will exhibit long leads on an inverted basis, and vice versa. Thus downturns in such "lagging indicators" as yields on new mortgages, unit-labor costs, and finished goods inventories all typically occur shortly after a business cycle peak has been reached. But these same reversals also frequently precede and in some degree give rise to upturns in such "leading indicators" as housing starts, profit margins, and investment in purchased materials inventories. In this sense, the lagging indicators are among the longest leading indicators.

This instructive way of reversing the order of these types of series was recognized in both the 1938 and the 1950 NBER studies of indicators. In the 1938 study, three series on bond yields were listed among those with the longest lags, but the same series, analyzed on an inverted basis, were also listed among those with the longest leads. In the 1950 study, it was observed that the median trough in a group of lagging series had, during fifteen business cycles between 1885 and 1938, invariably preceded the median peak in a group of leading series. Also, the median peak in the lagging group had, with only one exception, always preceded the median trough in the leading group. The possibility that these sequences reflected causal connections among the indicators was noted.

These phenomena are a manifestation of the continuous round of developments that constitutes the business cycle. They are of vital significance for the business cycle analyst scrutinizing the interconnections between one economic process and another. The question of concern here is whether they can be recognized in a classification of indicators in such a way as to illuminate rather than confuse.[1]

3. A SHORT LIST OF INDICATORS

In each of the three preceding NBER studies of indicators, one of the ultimate products was a fairly short list of indicators: 21 in two studies, 26 in the third. In each case, also, longer lists were appended. The longer lists covered a broader array of economic activities, and also contained some duplication, where two or more series pertaining to a given type of activity complemented one another in some way. *Business Cycle Developments,* since its inception, has identified the series in the short list, and used an adaptation of it in certain charts and tables used to make cyclical comparisons. The short list has also been used in various compilations by private businesses. Are the purposes served by both a short and

[1] An experimental classification that recognized both length of lead and peak-trough differences was published in the National Bureau's 44th Annual Report, New York, June 1964, pp. 99–106. There the 52 indicators then classified in *Business Cycle Developments* as leading, roughly coincident, and lagging were reclassified into twelve groups that distinguish length of lead or lag and differences in timing at peaks and troughs. See also Edgar R. Fiedler, "Long-Lead and Short-Lead Indexes of Business Indicators," *Proceedings of the Business and Economic Statistics Section,* American Statistical Association, 1962.

a longer list sufficiently compelling to warrant their construction in the present review?

Let us describe briefly the principal differences between the short and long lists shown in *Business Cycle Developments* during 1966, consisting of 26 and 80 U.S. indicators respectively. First, the longer list includes 28 series that are not classified as leading, roughly coincident, or lagging indicators, but which nevertheless represent important factors in business cycles. Federal government receipts and expenditures, foreign trade, and various financial and other series are counted here. Some of these series have fairly recently been added to *Business Cycle Developments* and may deserve inclusion in one or another of the timing groups, but have not been so placed pending completion of the present review.

The remaining 52 series in the long list include, of course, the 26 in the short list and 26 others. Several of the latter had not been constructed or investigated at the time the short list was compiled in 1960. Examples are the ratio of wholesale prices to labor cost per unit of output in manufacturing, and the index of labor cost per dollar of real corporate gross national product. The rest are series closely related to those in the short list, but considered to have some disadvantages. An example is the number of persons on temporary layoff, which has a broader industrial coverage and is available more promptly than the layoff rate in manufacturing, but is far more erratic in its month-to-month movements. Another example is the insured unemployment rate, which is available weekly and is smoother than the total unemployment rate, but does not cover all the unemployed. A third example is the change in book value of manufacturing and trade inventories; this series is available monthly but has the conceptual disadvantage of being affected by inventory revaluation, unlike the quarterly GNP component, change in business inventories.

Hence the longer list contains data that are of definite value to the analyst despite their partial duplication of series in the short list. For some purposes, such as the construction of a monthly composite index based on the indicators, substitutions between the two lists may well be made.

One of the principal reasons why in former years a short list was needed has now become less pressing. With the publication of various private and governmental compilations weekly or monthly on a prompt schedule, the difficulties facing individuals, business firms, and other organizations who wish to keep a substantial collection of economic series up to date have greatly diminished. All the principal indicators are now available in seasonally adjusted form, thanks largely to the advent of electronic computer programs. Whereas fifteen years ago, keeping a list of even 25 indicators seasonally adjusted, up to date, and charted was a substantial burden, today that problem can be solved by the expenditure of a modest subscription fee. A short list is, therefore, no longer so essential for this reason.

Another important consideration, however, is that a short, substantially unduplicated list of principal indicators provides a way of summarizing the current situation and outlook. At least, it is a step toward a summary, from which one may wish to go farther or approach in different ways. The relations among 25 or 30 indicators are more comprehensible than those among two or three times that number. They can be conveyed to management or lay audiences with better hope of understanding. And they can be reviewed more quickly.

Moreover, if a short list were confined to monthly series, i.e., excluding quarterly, it would possess some other advantages. Monthly series are nearly always more up to date than quarterly. The uniformity in the time unit makes it easier to present and interpret tables showing recent changes, and to construct composite indexes based on the current data. Moreover, when such indexes are based on a relatively short list of components, it is easier to trace the proximate cause of their movements.

There are dangers, of course, in making

complicated matters too easy. It would not do, for example, to neglect quarterly series entirely. Gross national product, plant and equipment expenditures, new capital appropriations, change in business inventories, and corporate profits, all of which are quarterly, are far too important. Also, the analyst needs to check his observations and conclusions by inspecting different pieces of evidence, even though they partially duplicate one another. The estimates of nonagricultural employment from the establishment survey, for example, need to be compared with those from the labor force survey, the ratio of prices to unit labor costs needs to be checked against directly reported profit margins, and so on. Clearly, if we have a short list we also need a long list.

4. CLASSIFICATIONS BY TIMING AND BY ECONOMIC PROCESS

The indicators charted in *Business Cycle Developments* are grouped not only in leading, roughly coincident, and lagging categories but also in classes reflecting the kind of economic process they pertain to. Leading series have been classified as (1) sensitive employment and unemployment indicators, (2) new investment commitments, (3) new businesses and business failures, (4) profits and stock prices, and (5) inventory investment, buying policy, and sensitive prices. Similar but not identical economic-process headings appear in the roughly coincident and lagging groups. The purpose of this grouping was primarily to bring closely related series *within a given timing class* under one heading, so as to emphasize their interrelations.

An economic process grouping might also serve a somewhat different purpose. In analyzing business cycles it is necessary not only to examine different processes with substantially the same timing, such as profits and new investment commitments, or raw materials prices and inventory investment, but also to consider similar processes with significantly different timing, such as new investment commitments and actual investment outlays, or the average workweek and the number of persons employed, or unit labor costs and profit margins. These "within process" relationships are sometimes more readily accounted for and more easily comprehended than those between processes. In any case they are fundamental to a broad understanding of business cycles and they play an important role both in forecasting and in policymaking. For this reason, it has been deemed desirable to facilitate comparisons of series with different timing but pertaining to the same economic process by devising a classification adapted to that end.

It is not easy to accommodate the many purposes that a classification and presentation of indicators may serve, or to meet the varied interests and sophistication of the users, or to take into account both the simple and the intricate cyclical relationships among the series, some of which are well known and firmly established, others unfamiliar and perhaps ephemeral. A practical compromise is all that can be expected. The next section describes the compromises we have reached.

IV

The 1966 List of Indicators

1. GENERAL FRAMEWORK

The classification scheme devised for the 1966 list of indicators provides the following:

A. A list of series classified primarily by cyclical timing with a subclassification by economic process, this order being chosen because timing differences are of prime interest in short-run forecasting.[1] This list covers a broad range of economic activities with many closely related series that complement one another in various ways. It includes some series that do not move in close conformity to business cycles.

B. A short, unduplicated list of series, superior in quality as indicators and meeting high standards for conformity to business cycles, classified by timing alone. This set of data provides a convenient means of summarizing what the principal indicators reveal about the current situation and outlook, though the results need to be checked as well as amplified by reference to the full list.

C. A principal timing classification based on peak and trough behavior taken together, without reference to length of lead or lag. However, information is provided on timing at peaks and troughs separately, as well as on lengths of lead or lag (cf. Appendixes B and C).

D. An economic-process classification within each broad timing class that facilitates comparisons of similar economic activities with different timing as well as different economic activities with similar timing. The economic-process classes are the same as those used to evaluate economic significance (cf. Section 3, Chapter II).

2. THE FULL LIST

The new list, shown in Table 6 and Chart 1, includes 88 U.S. series: 36 leading, 25 roughly coincident, 11 lagging, and 16 unclassified by timing; 72 are monthly and 16 quarterly. In the previous list, shown in *Business Cycle Developments,* there were 80 U.S. series—30 leading, 15 coincident, 7 lagging, and 28 unclassified by timing. Table 6 shows the number of series within each of the timing and economic process categories in the new list.[2]

One objective of this list is to provide several closely related series for each type of activity having significance for business cycle analysis. Such "duplication" is desirable because some series appear at more frequent intervals and hence are more up to date than others that are conceptually more appropriate (price per unit of labor cost, available monthly, versus profits per dollar of sales, available quarterly); some appear more promptly but are less adequate statistically (percentage of purchasing agents reporting higher inventories of purchased materials versus actual reported changes in purchased materials inventories); some have sharper, more easily identified cyclical move-

[1] The use of timing as the primary basis of classification underscores the fact, important for forecasting, that many economic processes move more or less simultaneously with one another and in advance of others that also move more or less simultaneously with one another.

[2] Of the 72 series classified by timing, the separate peak and trough classifications show that 38 are in the same timing class at peaks and troughs, with 34 in different classes. These proportions do not differ much from those observed in the 1950 study.

ments but are not as comprehensive (labor income in mining, manufacturing, and construction versus total personal income); and some are smoother but less appropriate conceptually (housing permits versus housing starts). Thus, various series measuring similar activities complement one another in interpreting current business conditions and prospects. In general, the availability of closely related series facilitates the process of appraising the errors of measurement and other limitations of individual series, and obtaining a consensus among them.

Another type of duplication is also present in the list, namely, series that represent stocks as well as those that represent flows, or rates of change in the stock. For example, series on inventories as well as on inventory change, on debt outstanding as well as the net change in debt, on accessions and layoffs as well as on employment, are included. In general, the cyclical peaks and troughs in the flow are reached at earlier dates than those in the stock, so the series appear in different timing categories. We have restricted this kind of duplication to cases where some special significance attaches to both the flow and the stock and both score well as indicators.

The list includes 13 new series, that is, series not on the list appearing in *Business Cycle Developments* as of November 1966:

SERIES	EXPLANATION
Nonagricultural job openings, number pending	Best available series on job vacancies, with cyclical movements similar to those of help-wanted advertising. Its coverage is limited, however, to openings registered with U.S. Employment Service offices.
Change in mortgage debt	Most comprehensive monthly measure of the net volume of mortgage debt extended (residential and nonresidential). Represents, together with change in consumer instalment debt and in bank loans to business, one of the more cyclically volatile components of the flow of private debt.
Delinquency rate, instalment credit loans	One of the few promptly available measures of lending experience on consumer credit. Moves inversely with business cycles, often leading at peaks.
Man-hours, nonagricultural employment	Most comprehensive monthly measure of labor input. This series combines employment from the establishment survey with average hours worked from the labor force survey. The employment data from the establishment survey are used because of their better cyclical performance. The hours data from the labor force survey provide comprehensive industry coverage, but do not match precisely the establishment data.
Unemployment rate, fifteen weeks and over	Supplements other unemployment series, representing unemployment of longer duration and therefore of a more serious nature. Cyclical swings are wider than and lag behind those in the total unemployment rate. Thus it has confirmatory value as an indicator.
Machinery and equipment sales and business construction expenditures	Provides monthly estimates that correspond roughly to quarterly plant and equipment expenditures, and helps identify turning points in actual expenditures that may not appear in the anticipations data.

TAB

Eighty-eight Selected Indicators Classified by Timi

A. Individ

Classification and Series Title (1)	First Business Cycle Turn Covered (2)	Average Score: Series on Short List(*) (3a)	Average Score: Other Series (3b)	Scores, Six Criteria: Economic Significance (4)	Statistical Adequacy (5)	Conformity (6)	Timing (7)	Smoothness (8)	Cu ren (9
LEADING INDICAT									
1. Employment and unemployment									
Marginal employment adjustments									
*1. Avg. workweek, prod. workers, mfg.	1921	66		50	65	81	66	60	8
*30. Nonagri. placements, BES	1945	68		75	63	63	58	80	8
2. Accession rate, mfg.	1919		65	50	75	78	83	40	4
5. Initial claims, unempl. insur. (inv.)	1945		73	75	63	81	55	80	10
3. Layoff rate, mfg. (inv.)	1919		69	50	75	85	86	60	4
3. Fixed capital investment									
Formation of business enterprises									
*38. Index of net business formation	1945	68		75	58	81	67	80	
13. New business incorporations	1860		65	75	69	71	61	60	
New investment commitments									
*6. New orders, dur. goods indus.	1920	78		75	72	88	84	60	
94. Construction contracts, total, value	1910		59	75	78	45	66	20	
*10. Contracts and orders, plant and equip.	1948	64		75	63	92	50	40	
11. New capital appropriations, mfg., Q	1953		45	50	50	76	8	80	
24. New orders, mach. and equip. indus.	1948		72	50	68	92	82	60	
9. Constr. contracts, comm. and indus., floor area	1919		46	50	73	75	11	0	
7. Private nonfarm housing starts	1918		63	50	75	69	80	0	
*29. New building permits, private housing units	1918	67		50	60	76	80	60	
4. Inventories and inventory investment									
Inventory investment and purchasing									
21. Change in business inventories, all indus., Q	1921		61	75	75	81	28	40	
*31. Change in book value, mfg. and trade inventories	1945	65		75	67	77	78	20	
37. Purchased materials, % reptg. higher inventories	1948		62	50	58	76	55	60	
20. Change in bk. val., mfrs.' inventories of materials and supplies	1945		47	50	67	48	50	0	
26. Buying policy, mater., % reptg. commitments 60+ days	1953		62	50	51	66	71	60	
32. Vendor performance, % reptg. slower deliveries	1948		69	50	53	78	82	80	
25. Change in unfilled orders, dur. goods indus.	1945		68	50	67	81	82	40	
5. Prices, costs, and profits									
Sensitive commodity price indexes									
*23. Industrial materials prices	1919	67		50	72	79	44	80	1

...Economic Process: Scores and Timing Characteristics
...ies

	Timing at Peaks and Troughs					
...usi-ess cycle turns covered (10)	Leads (11)	Rough Coinci-dences[a] (12)	Lags (13)	Median Lead(−) or Lag(+) in Months (14)	Timing Class[c] (15)	Classification and Series Title (1)
...SERIES)						
						1. Employment and unemployment
						Marginal employment adjustments
9	13	4(2)	2	−5	L	*1. Avg. workweek, prod. workers, mfg.
0	8	4(0)	1	−3	L	*30. Nonagri. placements, BES
1	19	6(2)	0	−4	L	2. Accession rate, mfg.
0	6	4(2)	1	−6	L	5. Initial claims, unempl. insur. (inv.)
1	19	6(1)	0	−7	L	3. Layoff rate, mfg. (inv.)
						3. Fixed capital investment
						Formation of business enterprises
0	8	3(1)	0	−7	L	*38. Index of net business formation
0	33	13(2)	7	−5	L	13. New business incorporations
						New investment commitments
0	16	7(1)	0	−4	L	*6. New orders, dur. goods indus.
6	19	8(1)	1	−6	L	94. Construction contracts, total, value
8	7	2(0)	1	−6	L	*10. Contracts and orders, plant and equip.
6	4	3(0)	2	−4	L	11. New capital appropriations, mfg., Q
8	8	2(0)	0	−6	L	24. New orders, mach. and equip. indus.
[illegible]	11	8(1)	3	−2	L	9. Constr. contracts, comm. and indus., floor area
2	17	5(1)	1	−6	L	7. Private nonfarm housing starts
2	17	5(1)	1	−6	L	*29. New building permits, private housing units
						4. Inventories and inventory investment
						Inventory investment and purchasing
[illegible]	10	8(1)	8	−2	L	21. Change in business inventories, all indus., Q
[illegible]	9	2(1)	0	−8	L	*31. Change in book value, mfg. and trade inventories
[illegible]	6	3(1)	1	−4	L	37. Purchased materials, % reptg. higher inventories
[illegible]	8	4(0)	1	−6	L	20. Change in bk. val., mfrs.' inventories of materials and supplies
[illegible]	6	3(0)	0	−4	L	26. Buying policy, mater., % reptg. commitments 60+ days
[illegible]	8	1(0)	0	−8	L	32. Vendor performance, % reptg. slower deliveries
[illegible]	10	2(0)	0	−12	L	25. Change in unfilled orders, dur. goods indus.
						5. Prices, costs, and profits
						Sensitive commodity price indexes
	13	9(4)	2	−2	L	*23. Industrial materials prices

TABLE

Classification and Series Title (1)	First Business Cycle Turn Covered (2)	Average Score: Series on Short List(*) (3a)	Average Score: Other Series (3b)	Scores, Six Criteria: Economic Significance (4)	Statistical Adequacy (5)	Conformity (6)	Timing (7)	Smoothness (8)	Cu ren (9
									LEADING INDICAT
Stock price indexes									
*19. Stock prices, 500 common stocks	1873	81		75	74	77	87	80	10
Profits and profit margins									
*16. Corporate profits after taxes, Q	1920	68		75	70	79	76	60	2
22. Ratio, profits to income orig., corp., all indus., Q	1948		61	75	63	52	72	60	2
18. Profits per dollar of sales, corporate, mfg., Q	1948		58	50	63	74	72	60	
*17. Ratio, price to unit labor cost, mfg.	1919	69		50	67	84	72	60	8
6. Money and credit									
Flows of money and credit									
98. Change in money supply and time deposits[d]	1908		68	75	75	72	68	0	10
85. Change in money supply[d]	1914		70	75	75	89	63	0	10
110. Total private borrowing, Q	1953		60	75	67	88	39	60	
*113. Change in consumer instalment debt	1929	63		50	79	77	60	60	4
112. Change in bank loans to businesses	1938		53	50	47	65	41	20	10
33. Change in mortgage debt	1957		43	50	60	54	20	20	4
Credit difficulties									
14. Liabilities of business failures (inv.)	1879		68	75	74	86	66	0	8
39. Delinquency rate, instal. loans (inv.)	1948		59	50	73	72	50	60	4
									ROUGHLY COINCID
1. Employment and unemployment									
Job vacancies									
301. Nonagri. job openings, number pending, BES	1948		72	75	63	74	58	100	[illegible]
46. Help-wanted advertising	1919		76	75	60	96	58	100	[illegible]
Comprehensive employment series									
501. Man-hours in nonfarm establishments, employees	1945		71	75	60	89	52	80	[illegible]
*41. Employees in nonagri. establishments[e]	1929	81		75	61	90	87	100	[illegible]
42. Total nonagri. employment	1945		69	75	62	81	47	80	[illegible]
Comprehensive unemployment series									
*43. Unemployment rate, total (inv.)	1929	75		75	63	96	60	80	[illegible]
45. Insured unemployment rate (inv.)	1949		76	75	56	73	76	100	1[illegible]
40. Unemployment rate, married males (inv.)	1957		60	75	55	52	38	80	[illegible]
2. Production, income, consumption, and trade									
Comprehensive production series									
49. GNP in current dollars, expenditure estimate, Q	1921		80	75	75	92	82	100	

ontinued)

	Timing at Peaks and Troughs					
usi-ess ycle urns vered 10)	Leads (11)	Rough Coinci-dences[a] (12)	Lags (13)	Median Lead(−) or Lag(+) in Months (14)	Timing Class[c] (15)	Classification and Series Title (1)
CLUDED)						
						Stock price indexes
44	33	14(2)	5	−4	L	*19. Stock prices, 500 common stocks
						Profits and profit margins
20	13	11(4)	2	−2	L	*16. Corporate profits after taxes, Q
8	7	2(1)	0	−7	L	22. Ratio, profits to income orig., corp., all indus., Q
8	7	3(1)	0	−7	L	18. Profits per dollar of sales, corporate, mfg., Q
21	17	10(1)	3	−3	L	*17. Ratio, price to unit labor cost, mfg.
						6. Money and credit
						Flows of money and credit
27	24	0(0)	1	−15	L	98. Change in money supply and time deposits[d]
23	19	1(0)	1	−14	L	85. Change in money supply[d]
6	4	2(1)	1	−8	L	110. Total private borrowing, Q
14	11	4(0)	1	−10	L	*113. Change in consumer instalment debt
11	6	4(2)	1	−4	L	112. Change in bank loans to businesses
4	3	1(1)	0	−8	L	33. Change in mortgage debt
						Credit difficulties
43	31	5(2)	3	−7	L	14. Liabilities of business failures (inv.)
8	6	5(0)	2	−3	L	39. Delinquency rate, instal. loans (inv.)
CATORS (25 SERIES)						
						1. Employment and unemployment
						Job vacancies
8	3	4(2)	2	0	C(U)	301. Nonagri. job openings, number pending, BES
1	6	14(7)	6	0	C	46. Help-wanted advertising
						Comprehensive employment series
0	6	8(2)	2	−1	C	501. Man-hours in nonfarm establishments, employees
4	6	12(6)	2	0	C	*41. Employees in nonagri. establishments[e]
0	7	7(1)	2	−2	C(L)	42. Total nonagri. employment
						Comprehensive unemployment series
4	4	8(3)	6	0	C	*43. Unemployment rate, total (inv.)
7	3	5(2)	2	0	C	45. Insured unemployment rate (inv.)
4	2	2(0)	2	−4	C(U)	40. Unemployment rate, married males (inv.)
						2. Production, income, consumption, and trade
						Comprehensive production series
9	6	14(3)	6	0	C	49. GNP in current dollars, expenditure estimate, Q

TABLE

Classification and Series Title (1)	First Business Cycle Turn Covered (2)	Average Score: Series on Short List(*) (3a)	Average Score: Other Series (3b)	Scores, Six Criteria: Economic Significance (4)	Statistical Adequacy (5)	Conformity (6)	Timing (7)	Smoothness (8)	Currenc (9)
									ROUGHLY COINCIDE
*50. GNP in constant dollars, expenditure estimate, Q	1921	73		75	75	91	58	80	50
*47. Industrial production[f]	1919	72		75	63	94	38	100	80
Comprehensive income series									
*52. Personal income	1921	74		75	73	89	43	100	80
53. Labor income in mining, mfg., and constr.	1929		77	50	69	94	81	100	80
Comprehensive consumption and trade series									
57. Final sales in current dollars, Q	1921		66	75	78	77	26	100	50
*816. Mfg. and trade sales	1948	71		75	68	70	80	80	40
*54. Sales of retail stores	1919	69		75	77	89	12	80	100
3. Fixed capital investment									
Backlog of investment commitments									
96. Mfrs.' unfilled orders, dur. goods indus.	1945		70	50	67	77	64	100	80
97. Backlog of cap. appropriations, mfg., Q	1953		54	50	50	74	44	100	[illegible]
5. Prices, costs, and profits									
Comprehensive wholesale price indexes									
55. Wholesale prices exc. farm products and foods	1913		67	75	72	86	12	100	8
58. Wholesale price index, mfd. goods	1913		59	50	72	73	8	100	8
6. Money and credit									
Money market interest rates									
114. Treasury bill rate	1920		67	50	77	92	28	80	10
116. Corporate bond yields	1948		57	50	56	92	19	40	10
115. Treasury bond yields	1919		63	50	73	75	25	80	10
117. Municipal bond yields[g]	1919		57	50	70	52	35	60	10
Bank reserves									
93. Free reserves (inv.)[h]	1929		60	75	59	80	5	60	10
									LAGGING INDICATO
1. Employment and unemployment									
Long-duration unemployment									
*502. Unempl. rate, persons unempl. 15+ weeks (inv.)	1948	69		50	63	98	52	80	8
3. Fixed capital investment									
Investment expenditures									
*61. Bus. expend., new plant and equip., Q	1918	86		75	77	96	94	100	8
505. Mach. and equip. sales and bus. constr. expend.	1948		68	75	56	92	58	80	4
4. Inventories and inventory investment									
Inventories									
*71. Book value, mfg. and trade inventories	1945	71		75	67	75	66	100	4

Continued)

Business Cycle Turns overed (10)	Leads (11)	Rough Coincidences[a] (12)	Lags (13)	Median Lead(−) or Lag(+) in Months (14)	Timing Class[c] (15)	Classification and Series Title (1)
Timing at Peaks and Troughs						
DICATORS (CONCLUDED)						
17	7	9(3)	3	−2	C(U)	*50. GNP in constant dollars, expenditure estimate, Q
21	9	13(9)	3	0	C	*47. Industrial production[f]
						Comprehensive income series
19	10	12(2)	5	−1	C	*52. Personal income
14	4	12(6)	4	0	C	53. Labor income in mining, mfg., and constr.
						Comprehensive consumption and trade series
19	6	7(0)	9	+3	C(U)	57. Final sales in current dollars, Q
8	4	6(4)	0	0	C	*816. Mfg. and trade sales
21	5	7(1)	6	0	C(U)	*54. Sales of retail stores
						3. Fixed capital investment
						Backlog of investment commitments
10	6	4(1)	3	−3	C(L)	96. Mfrs.' unfilled orders, dur. goods indus.
6	2	2(0)	3	+3	C(U)	97. Backlog of cap. appropriations, mfg., Q
						5. Prices, costs, and profits
						Comprehensive wholesale price indexes
24	2	10(2)	9	+1	C(U)	55. Wholesale prices exc. farm products and foods
24	7	7(1)	7	0	C(U)	58. Wholesale price index, mfd. goods
						6. Money and credit
						Money market interest rates
20	10	10(0)	6	−1	C(U)	114. Treasury bill rate
8	4	4(0)	4	0	C(U)	116. Corporate bond yields
21	7	9(3)	8	0	C(U)	115. Treasury bond yields
21	7	8(1)	13	+2	C(Lg)	117. Municipal bond yields[g]
						Bank reserves
14	5	6(1)	3	−1	C(U)	93. Free reserves (inv.)[h]
SERIES)						
						1. Employment and unemployment
						Long-duration unemployment
8	1	5(1)	6	+2	Lg	*502. Unempl. rate, persons unempl. 15+ weeks (inv.)
						3. Fixed capital investment
						Investment expenditures
20	2	16(5)	13	+1	Lg(C)	*61. Bus. expend., new plant and equip., Q
8	2	7(0)	6	+2	Lg	505. Mach. and equip. sales and bus. constr. expend.
						4. Inventories and inventory investment
						Inventories
10	2	7(0)	8	+2	Lg	*71. Book value, mfg. and trade inventories

TABLI

Classification and Series Title (1)	First Business Cycle Turn Covered (2)	Average Score: Series on Short List(*) (3a)	Average Score: Other Series (3b)	Scores, Six Criteria: Economic Significance (4)	Statistical Adequacy (5)	Conformity (6)	Timing (7)	Smoothness (8)	Cu ren (9
LAGGING INDICAT									
65. Book value of mfrs.' inventories, finished goods	1938		65	50	63	72	68	100	4
5. Prices, costs, and profits									
Unit labor costs									
68. Labor cost per dollar of real corp. GNP, Q[i]	1948		67	75	63	88	56	80	2
*62. Labor cost per unit of output, mfg.[i]	1919	68		50	70	83	56	80	8
6. Money and credit									
Outstanding debt									
66. Consumer instalment debt	1929		51	50	79	24	32	100	4
*72. Comm. and indus. loans outstanding	1937	57		50	47	67	20	100	10
Interest rates on business loans and mortgages									
*67. Bank rates on short-term bus. loans, Q[i]	1919	60		50	55	82	47	80	5
118. Mortgage yields, residential[i]	1948		55	50	43	70	24	100	8
OTHER SELEC									
5. Prices, costs, and profits									
Comprehensive retail price indexes									
81. Consumer price index	1913		45	75	50	20	12	100	4
7. Foreign trade and payments									
89. U.S. balance of payments, Q	1945		49	75	63	64	10	40	2
88. Merchandise trade balance (inv.)	1867		53	75	72	64	6	60	4
86. Exports, exc. military aid	1867		39	75	72	4	6	40	4
861. Export orders, durable goods	j		n.a.	50	53	n.a.	n.a.	0	4
862. Export orders, machinery	1957		n.a.	50	45	n.a.	n.a.	60	4
87. General imports	1867		53	75	75	67	9	40	4
8. Federal government activities									
95. Fed. surplus or deficit, income and prod. acct., Q	1948		60	75	63	77	44	60	2
84. Fed. cash surplus or deficit	1879		56	75	65	84	4	20	8
83. Fed. cash receipts from public	1879		56	75	65	94	8	0	8
82. Fed. cash payments to public	1879		38	75	69	6	2	0	8
101. Natl. defense purch., GNP component, current dollars, Q	1948		39	50	68	4	9	80	5
91. Defense Dept. oblig., total	1953		44	50	57	52	40	0	4
90. Defense Dept. oblig., procurement	1953		45	50	57	56	40	0	4
99. New orders, defense products	1953		40	50	62	30	19	0	8
92. Military contract awards in U.S.	1953		45	50	46	66	44	0	4

Continued)

Business Cycle Turns Covered (10)	Leads (11)	Rough Coincidences[a] (12)	Lags (13)	Median Lead(−) or Lag(+) in Months (14)	Timing Class[c] (15)	Classification and Series Title (1)
NCLUDED)						
11	2	3(0)	9	+5	Lg	65. Book value of mfrs.' inventories, finished goods
						5. Prices, costs, and profits
						Unit labor costs
8	1	1(0)	7	+7	Lg	68. Labor cost per dollar of real corp. GNP, Q[i]
21	0	1(0)	14	+8	Lg	*62. Labor cost per unit of output, mfg.[i]
						6. Money and credit
						Outstanding debt
14	1	4(0)	9	+4	Lg	66. Consumer instalment debt
12	1	6(0)	7	+2	Lg	*72. Comm. and indus. loans outstanding
						Interest rates on business loans and mortgages
21	2	5(1)	15	+5	Lg	*67. Bank rates on short-term bus. loans, Q[i]
8	1	3(0)	6	+4	Lg	118. Mortgage yields, residential[i]
RIES (16 SERIES)						
						5. Prices, costs, and profits
						Comprehensive retail price indexes
24	2	5(1)	11	+4	U	81. Consumer price index
						7. Foreign trade and payments
10	3	1(0)	1	−4	U	89. U.S. balance of payments, Q
47	14	16(4)	13	0	U	88. Merchandise trade balance (inv.)
47	9	6(2)	9	0	U	86. Exports, exc. military aid
	no timing comparisons				U	861. Export orders, durable goods
4	0	0(0)	1	+4[k]	U	862. Export orders, machinery
47	17	23(4)	16	0	U	87. General imports
						8. Federal government activities
8	5	2(0)	3	−6	U(L)	95. Fed. surplus or deficit, income and prod. acct., Q
43	15	13(3)	17	0	U	84. Fed. cash surplus or deficit
43	15	17(7)	14	0	U	83. Fed. cash receipts from public
43	10	7(2)	9	0	U	82. Fed. cash payments to public
8	1	1(0)	3	+6	U	101. Natl. defense purch., GNP component, current dollars, Q
6	5	0(0)	0	−11	U(L)	91. Defense Dept. oblig., total
6	5	0(0)	0	−11	U(L)	90. Defense Dept. oblig., procurement
6	3	0(0)	0	−11	U	99. New orders, defense products
6	5	0(0)	0	−10	U(L)	92. Military contract awards in U.S.

TABLE
B. Gro

Economic Process and Number of Series in Group (1)	Average of Average Score (2)	Average of Scores, Six Criteria: Economic Significance (3)	Statistical Adequacy (4)	Conformity (5)	Timing (6)	Smoothness (7)	Cu renc (8)
LEADI							
Marginal employment adjustments (5)	68	60	68	78	70	64	6
Formation of business enterprises (2)	66	75	64	76	64	70	4
New investment commitments (8)	62	59	67	77	58	40	5
Inventory investment and purchasing (7)	62	57	63	72	64	43	64
Sensitive commodity price indexes (1)	67	50	72	79	44	80	10
Stock price indexes (1)	81	75	74	77	87	80	10
Profits and profit margins (4)	64	62	66	72	73	60	3
Flows of money and credit (6)	60	62	67	74	48	27	6
Credit difficulties (2)	64	62	74	79	58	30	6
ROUGHLY COINDI							
Job vacancies (2)	74	75	62	85	58	100	8
Comprehensive employment series (3)	74	75	61	87	62	87	8
Comprehensive unemployment series (3)	70	75	58	74	58	87	8
Comprehensive production series (3)	75	75	71	92	59	93	6
Comprehensive income series (2)	76	62	71	92	62	100	8
Comprehensive consumption and trade series (3)	69	75	74	79	39	87	6
Backlog of investment commitments (2)	62	50	58	76	54	100	4
Comprehensive wholesale price indexes (2)	63	62	72	80	10	100	8
Money market interest rates (4)	61	50	69	78	27	65	10
Bank reserves (1)	60	75	59	80	5	60	10
LAGGI							
Long-duration unemployment (1)	69	50	63	98	52	80	8
Investment expenditures (2)	77	75	66	94	76	90	6
Inventories (2)	68	62	65	74	67	100	4
Unit labor costs (2)	68	62	66	86	56	80	5
Outstanding debt (2)	54	50	63	46	26	100	7
Interest rates on business loans and mortgages (2)	58	50	49	76	36	90	6
OTHER SELECT							
Comprehensive retail price indexes (1)	45	75	50	20	12	100	4
Foreign trade and payments (4)[l]	48	75	70	50	8	45	3
Federal government activities (9)	47	61	61	52	23	18	5

* On short list of indicators (25 series).

[a] Rough coincidences include exact coincidences (shown in parentheses) and leads and lags of 3 months or l
Leads (lags) include leads (lags) of 1 month or more. The total number of timing comparisons, which can be
than the number of business cycles covered by the series, is the sum of the leads, exact coincidences, and lags. Le
and lags of quarterly series are expressed in terms of months.

[b] Median for the group is the median of the medians for the individual series.

[c] L = leading; C = roughly coincident; Lg = lagging; U = unclassified by timing. The classification is ba
on the median lead or lag plus a probability test applied to the number of leads, rough coincidences, or lags rela
to the number of business cycle turns covered (see text). Where the final designated class differs from that obtai
by application of this rule, the latter is shown in parentheses.

ontinued)
mmaries

	Timing at Peaks and Troughs								
Total Number of				% of Business Cycle Turns					
usi- ness ycle urns ov- ered (9)	Leads (10)	Rough Coinci- dences[a] (11)	Lags (12)	Leads (13)	Rough Coinci- dences[a] (14)	Lags (15)	Median Lead(−) or Lag(+) in Mos.[b] (16)	Tim- ing Class[c] (17)	Economic Process and Number of Series in Group (1)
ICATORS									
81	65	24(7)	4	80	30(9)	5	−5	L	Marginal employment adjustments (5)
60	41	16(3)	7	68	27(5)	12	−6	L	Formation of business enterprises (2)
133	99	40(5)	9	74	30(4)	7	−6	L	New investment commitments (8)
71	57	23(3)	10	80	32(4)	14	−6	L	Inventory investment and purchasing (7)
21	13	9(4)	2	62	43(19)	10	−2	L	Sensitive commodity price indexes (1)
44	33	14(2)	5	75	32(5)	11	−4	L	Stock price indexes (1)
57	44	26(7)	5	77	46(12)	9	−5	L	Profits and profit margins (4)
85	67	12(4)	5	79	14(5)	6	−9	L	Flows of money and credit (6)
51	37	10(2)	5	73	20(4)	10	−5	L	Credit difficulties (2)
ICATORS									
29	9	18(9)	8	31	62(31)	28	0	C	Job vacancies (2)
34	19	27(9)	6	56	79(26)	18	−1	C	Comprehensive employment series (3)
25	9	15(5)	10	36	60(20)	40	0	C	Comprehensive unemployment series (3)
57	22	36(15)	12	39	63(26)	21	0	C	Comprehensive production series (3)
33	14	24(8)	9	42	73(24)	27	0	C	Comprehensive income series (2)
48	15	20(5)	15	31	42(10)	31	0	C(U)	Comprehensive consumption and trade series (3)
16	8	6(1)	6	50	38(6)	38	0	C(U)	Backlog of investment commitments (2)
48	9	17(3)	16	19	35(6)	33	0	C(U)	Comprehensive wholesale price indexes (2)
70	28	31(4)	31	40	44(6)	44	0	C(U)	Money market interest rates (4)
14	5	6(1)	3	36	43(7)	21	−1	C(U)	Bank reserves (1)
ICATORS									
8	1	5(1)	6	12	62(12)	75	+2	Lg	Long-duration unemployment (1)
28	4	23(5)	19	14	82(18)	68	+2	Lg	Investment expenditures (2)
21	4	10(0)	17	19	48(0)	81	+4	Lg	Inventories (2)
29	1	2(0)	21	3	7(0)	72	+8	Lg	Unit labor costs (2)
26	2	10(0)	16	8	38(0)	62	+3	Lg	Outstanding debt (2)
29	3	8(1)	21	10	28(3)	72	+4	Lg	Interest rates on business loans and mortgages (2)
IES									
24	2	5(1)	11	8	21(4)	46	+4	U	Comprehensive retail price indexes (1)
151	43	46(10)	39	28	30(7)	26	0	U	Foreign trade and payments (4)[l]
169	64	40(12)	46	38	24(7)	27	−6	U	Federal government activities (9)

Also analyzed invertedly, in which case the series is classed as lagging.
Earlier segment omitted, 1914–28 (production worker employment).
Earlier segment omitted, 1890–1918 (volume of business activity, Babson).
Earlier segment omitted, 1857–1918.
Also analyzed positively, in which case the series is classed as lagging.
Also analyzed invertedly, in which case the series is classed as leading.
Data not available before October 1962.
Based on fewer than 3 timing observations.
Two series (export orders, durable goods and export orders, machinery) omitted because complete set of measures is not ilable.

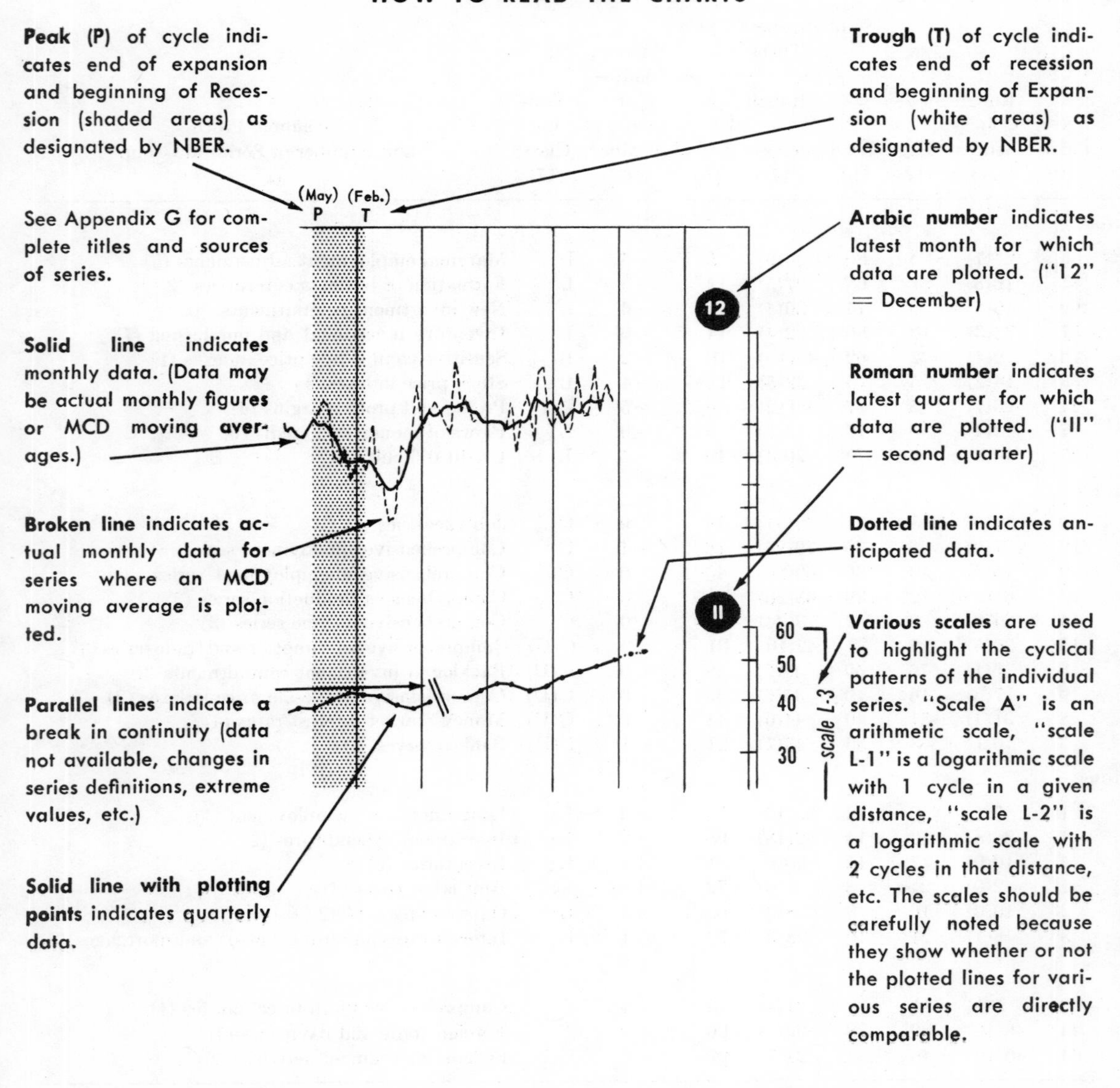
HOW TO READ THE CHARTS
Peak (P) of cycle indicates end of expansion and beginning of Recession (shaded areas) as designated by NBER.
Trough (T) of cycle indicates end of recession and beginning of Expansion (white areas) as designated by NBER.
(May) (Feb.)
P T
See Appendix G for complete titles and sources of series.
Arabic number indicates latest month for which data are plotted. ("12" = December)
12
Solid line indicates monthly data. (Data may be actual monthly figures or MCD moving averages.)
Roman number indicates latest quarter for which data are plotted. ("II" = second quarter)
Broken line indicates actual monthly data for series where an MCD moving average is plotted.
Dotted line indicates anticipated data.
II
60
50
40
30
scale L-3
Various scales are used to highlight the cyclical patterns of the individual series. "Scale A" is an arithmetic scale, "scale L-1" is a logarithmic scale with 1 cycle in a given distance, "scale L-2" is a logarithmic scale with 2 cycles in that distance, etc. The scales should be carefully noted because they show whether or not the plotted lines for various series are directly comparable.
Parallel lines indicate a break in continuity (data not available, changes in series definitions, extreme values, etc.)
Solid line with plotting points indicates quarterly data.

CHART 1

Eighty-eight Selected Indicators Classified by Timing and Economic Process

Leading Indicators, 36 Series

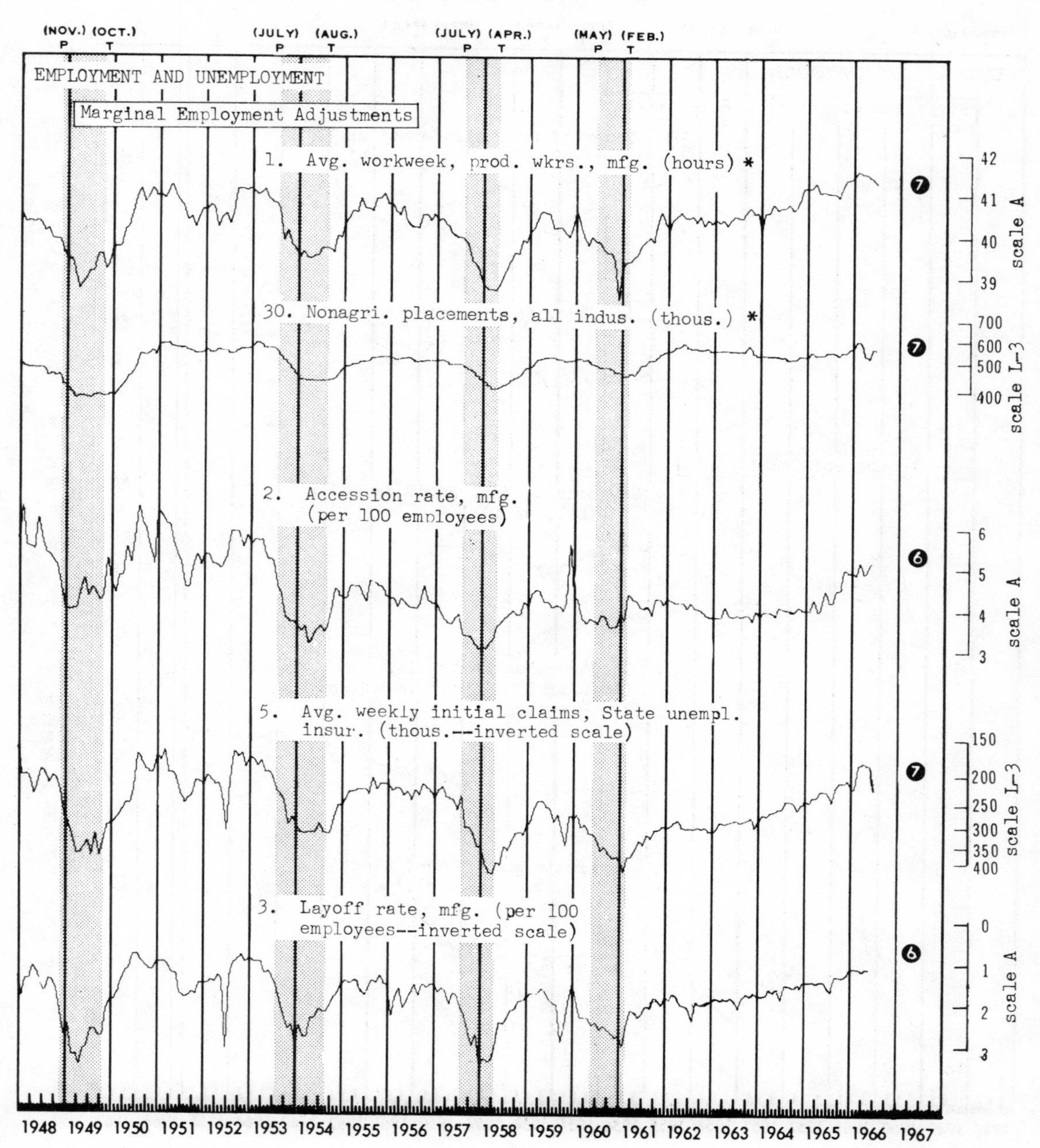

* Short list.

Note: Numbers in the dark circles indicate latest month plotted.

CHART 1

Eighty-eight Selected Indicators Classified by Timing and Economic Process

Leading Indicators, 36 Series (Continued)

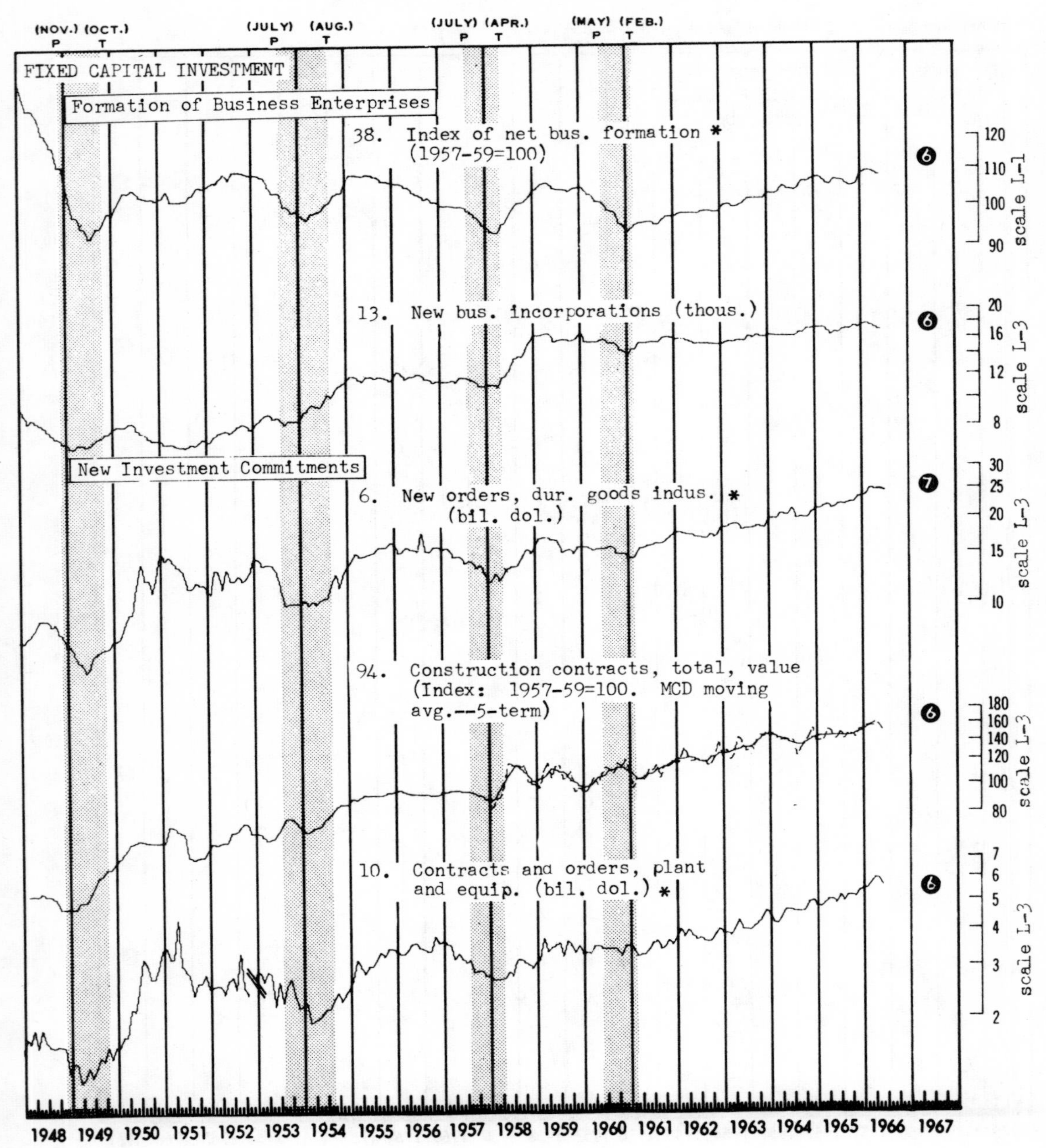

CHART 1

Eighty-eight Selected Indicators Classified by Timing and Economic Process

Leading Indicators, 36 Series (Continued)

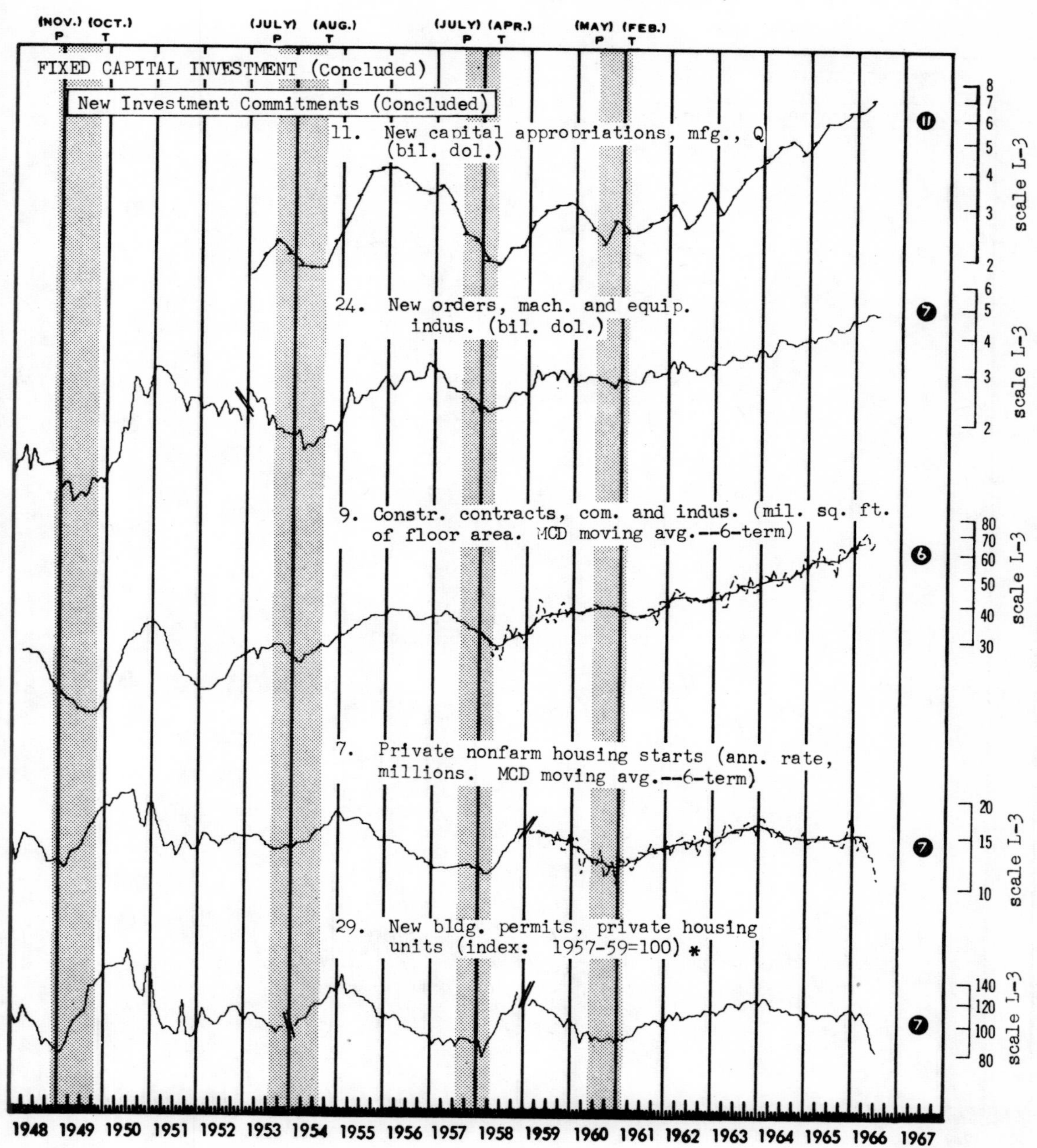

CHART 1

Eighty-eight Selected Indicators Classified by Timing and Economic Process

Leading Indicators, 36 Series (Continued)

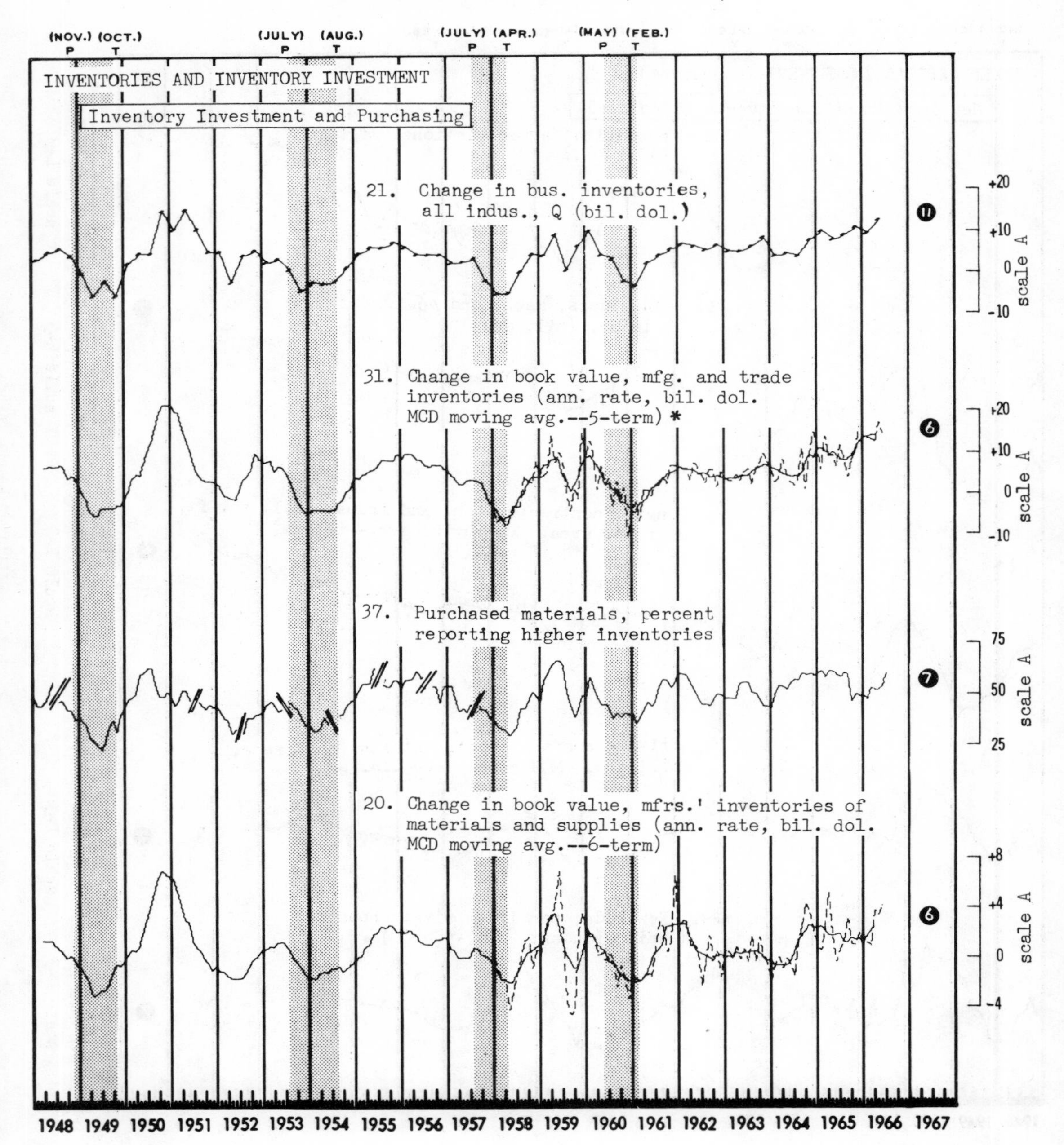

CHART 1

Eighty-eight Selected Indicators Classified by Timing and Economic Process

Leading Indicators, 36 Series (Continued)

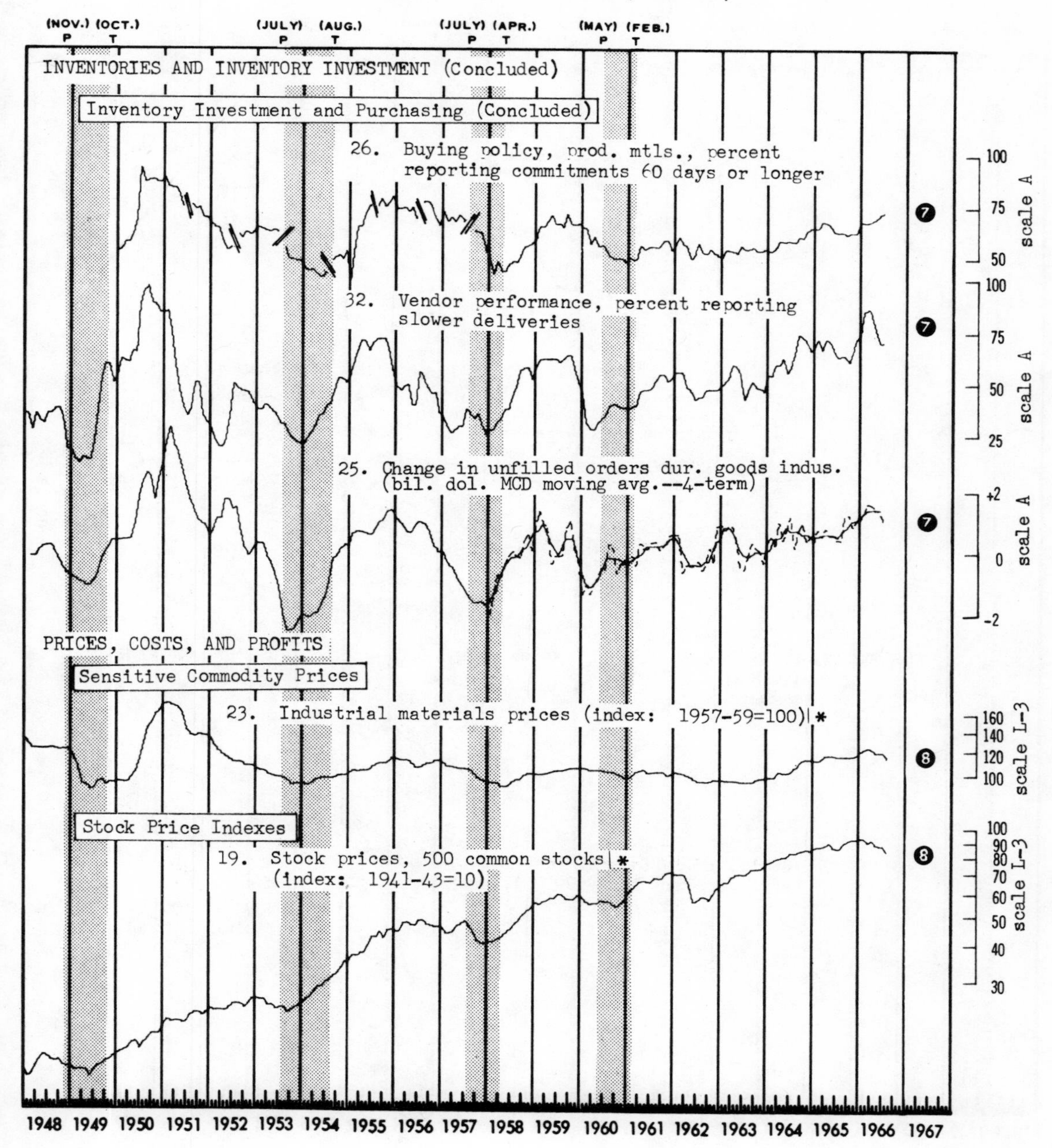

CHART 1

Eighty-eight Selected Indicators Classified by Timing and Economic Process

Leading Indicators, 36 Series (Continued)

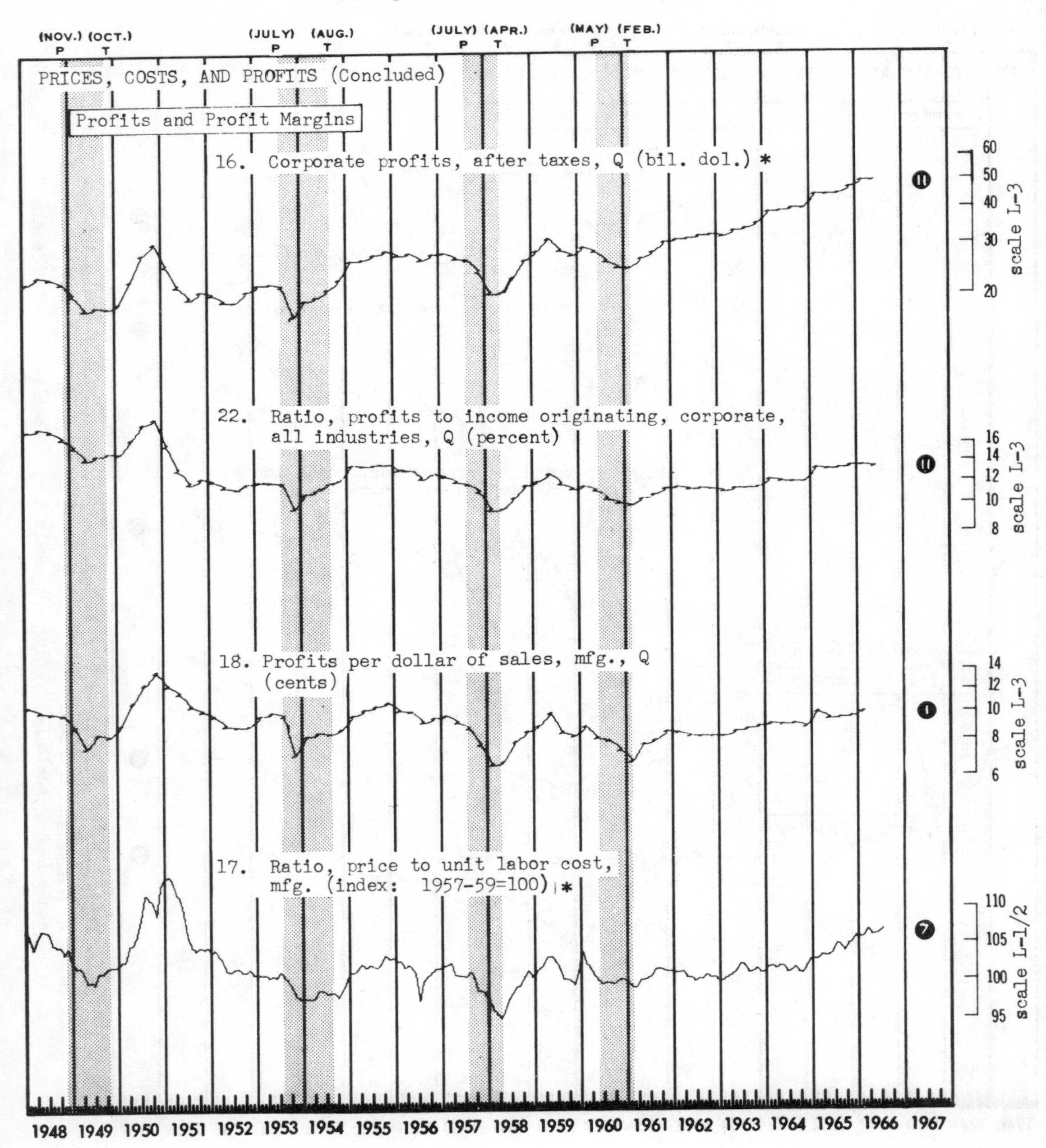

CHART 1

Eighty-eight Selected Indicators Classified by Timing and Economic Process

Leading Indicators, 36 Series (Continued)

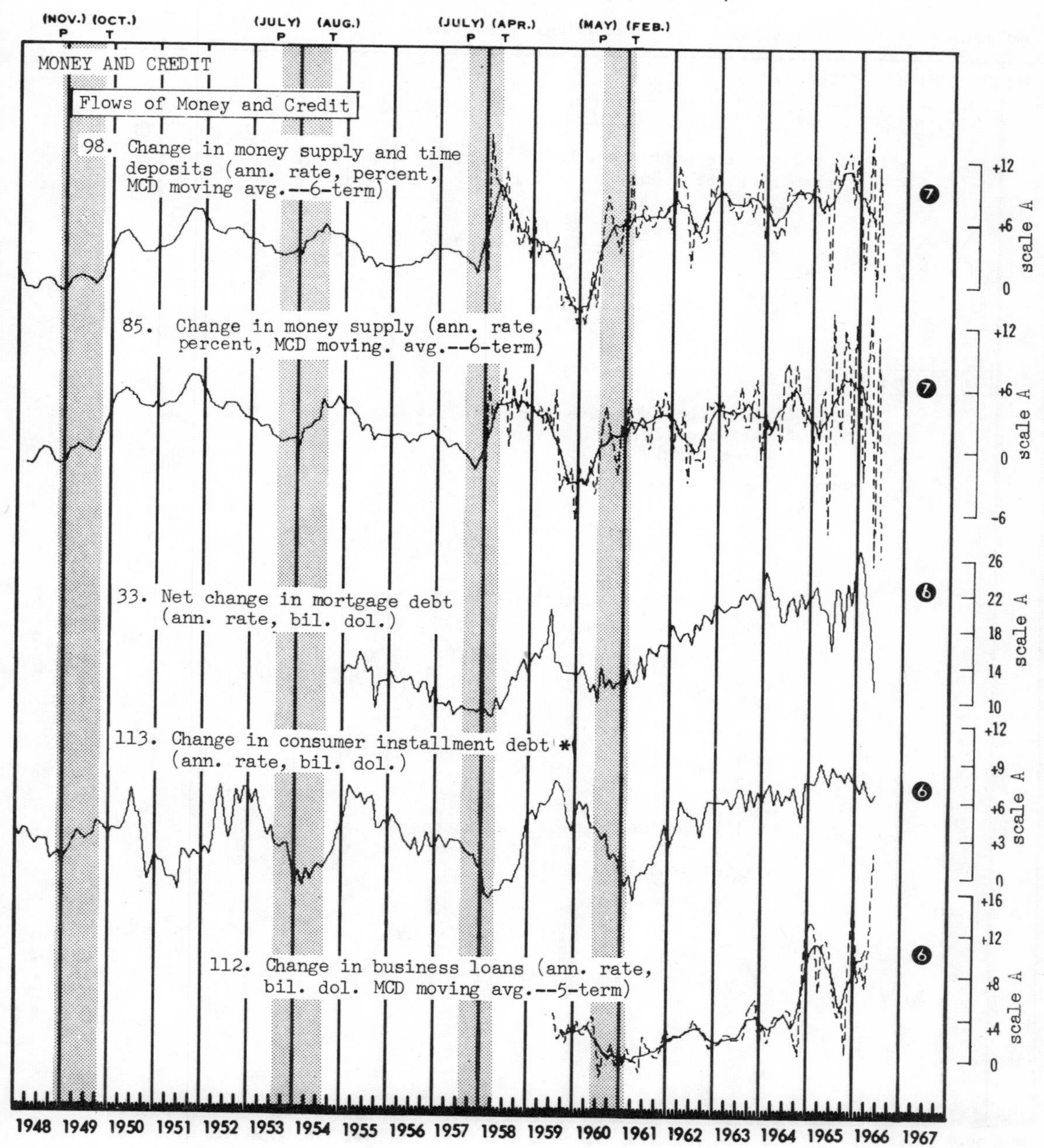

CHART 1

Eighty-eight Selected Indicators Classified by Timing and Economic Process

Leading Indicators, 36 Series (Concluded)

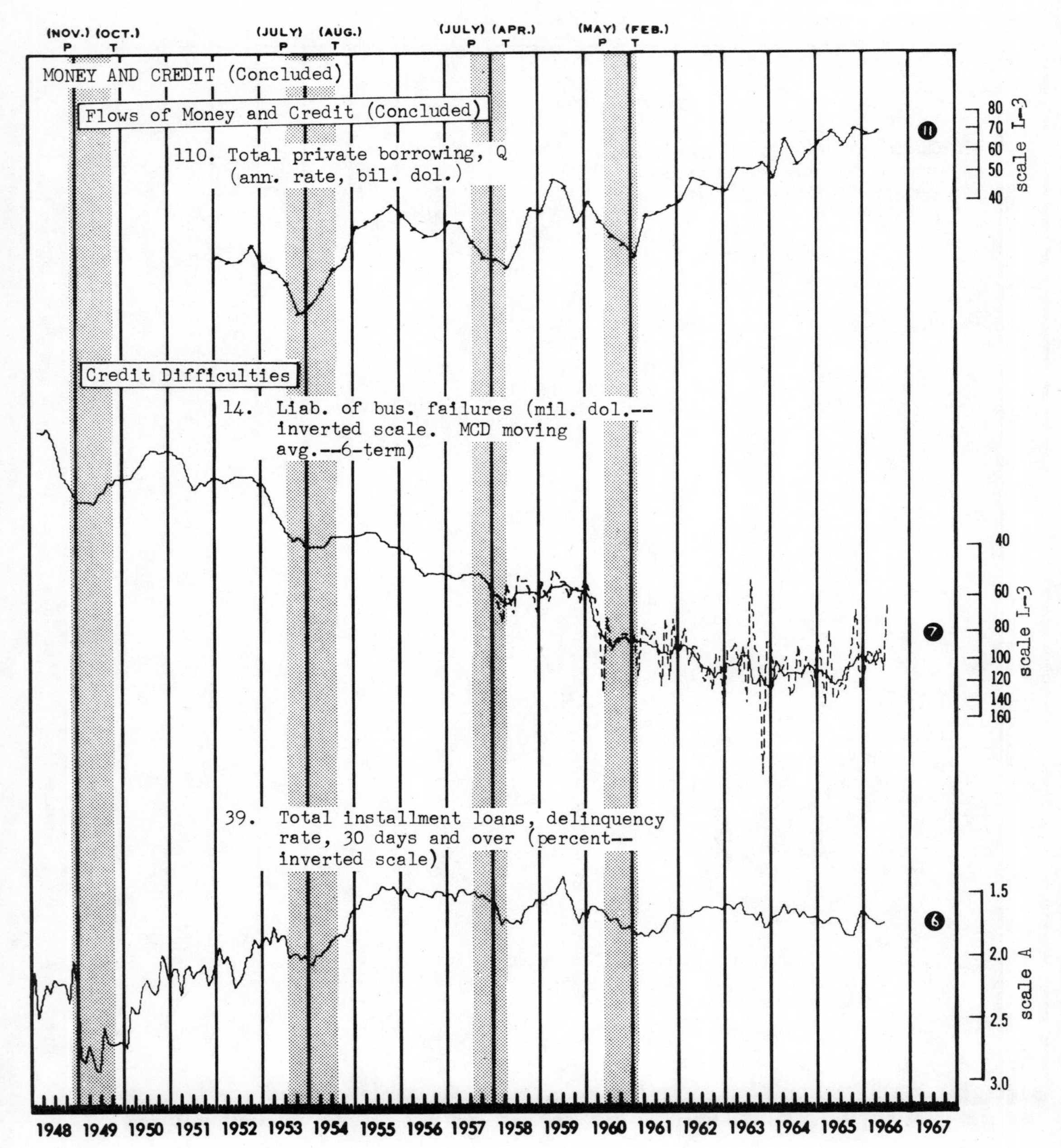

CHART 1

Eighty-eight Selected Indicators Classified by Timing and Economic Process

Roughly Coincident Indicators, 25 Series

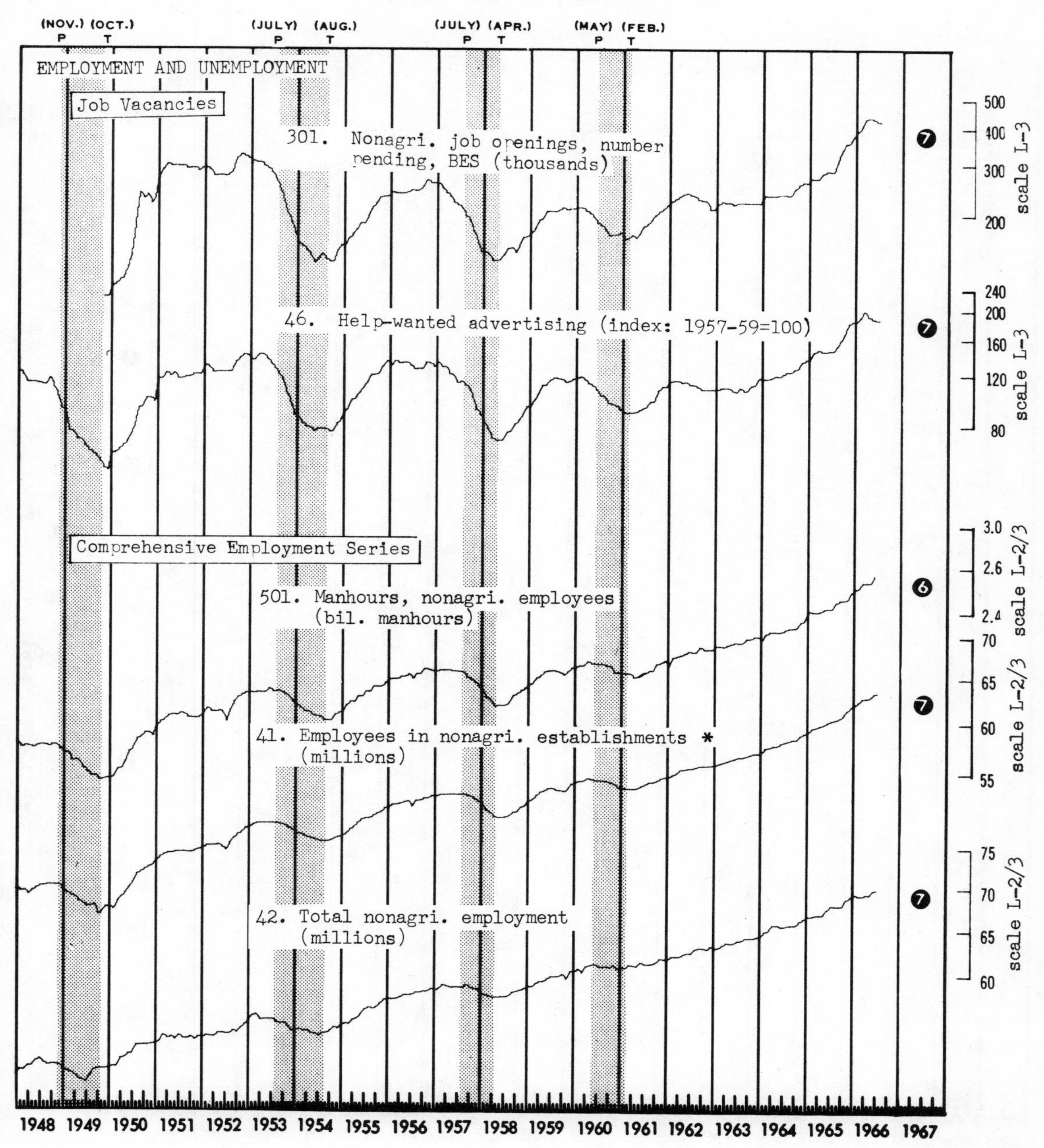

CHART 1

Eighty-eight Selected Indicators Classified by Timing and Economic Process

Roughly Coincident Indicators, 25 Series (Continued)

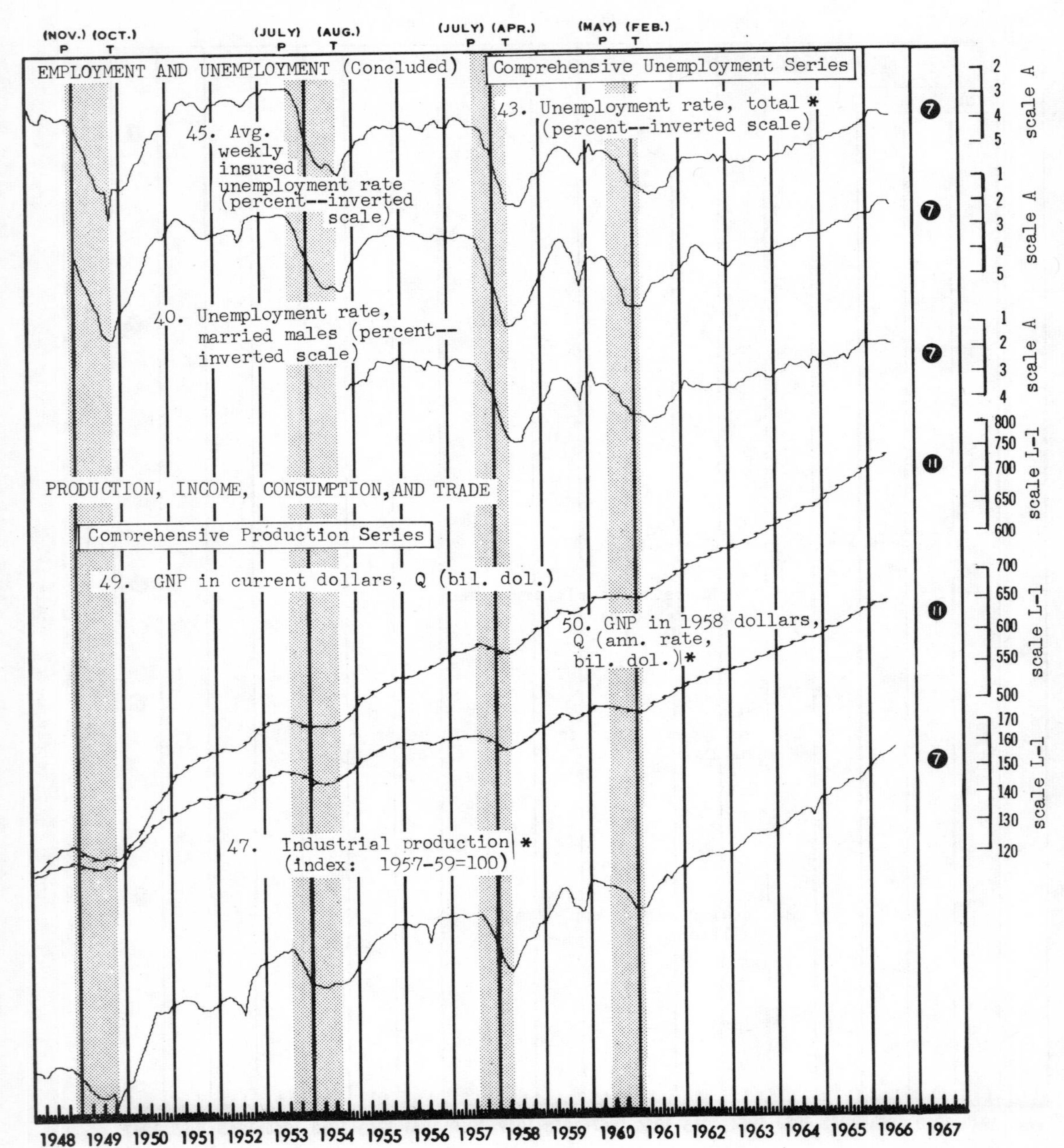

CHART 1

Eighty-eight Selected Indicators Classified by Timing and Economic Process

Roughly Coincident Indicators, 25 Series (Continued)

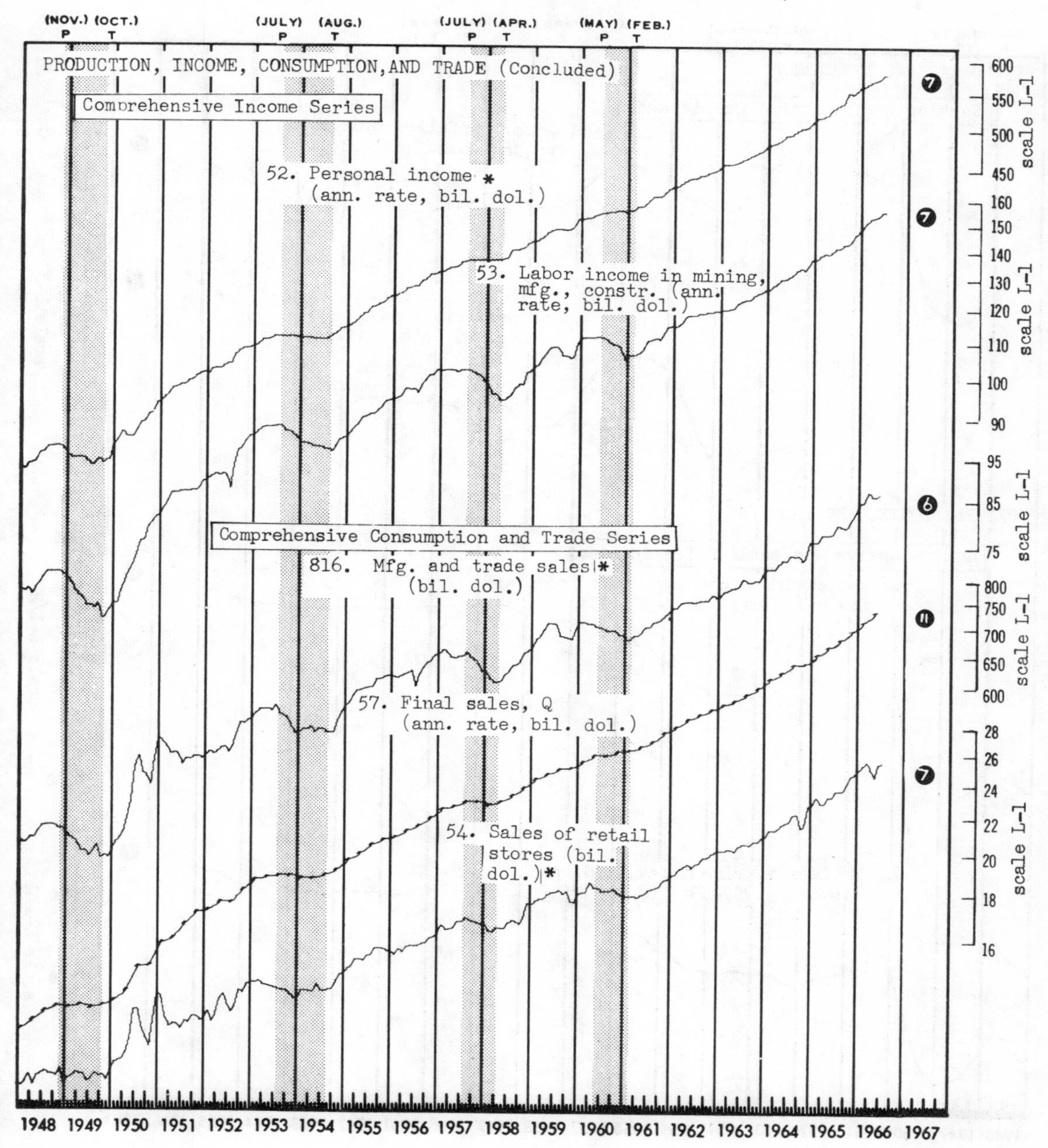

CHART 1

Eighty-eight Selected Indicators Classified by Timing and Economic Process

Roughly Coincident Indicators, 25 Series (Continued)

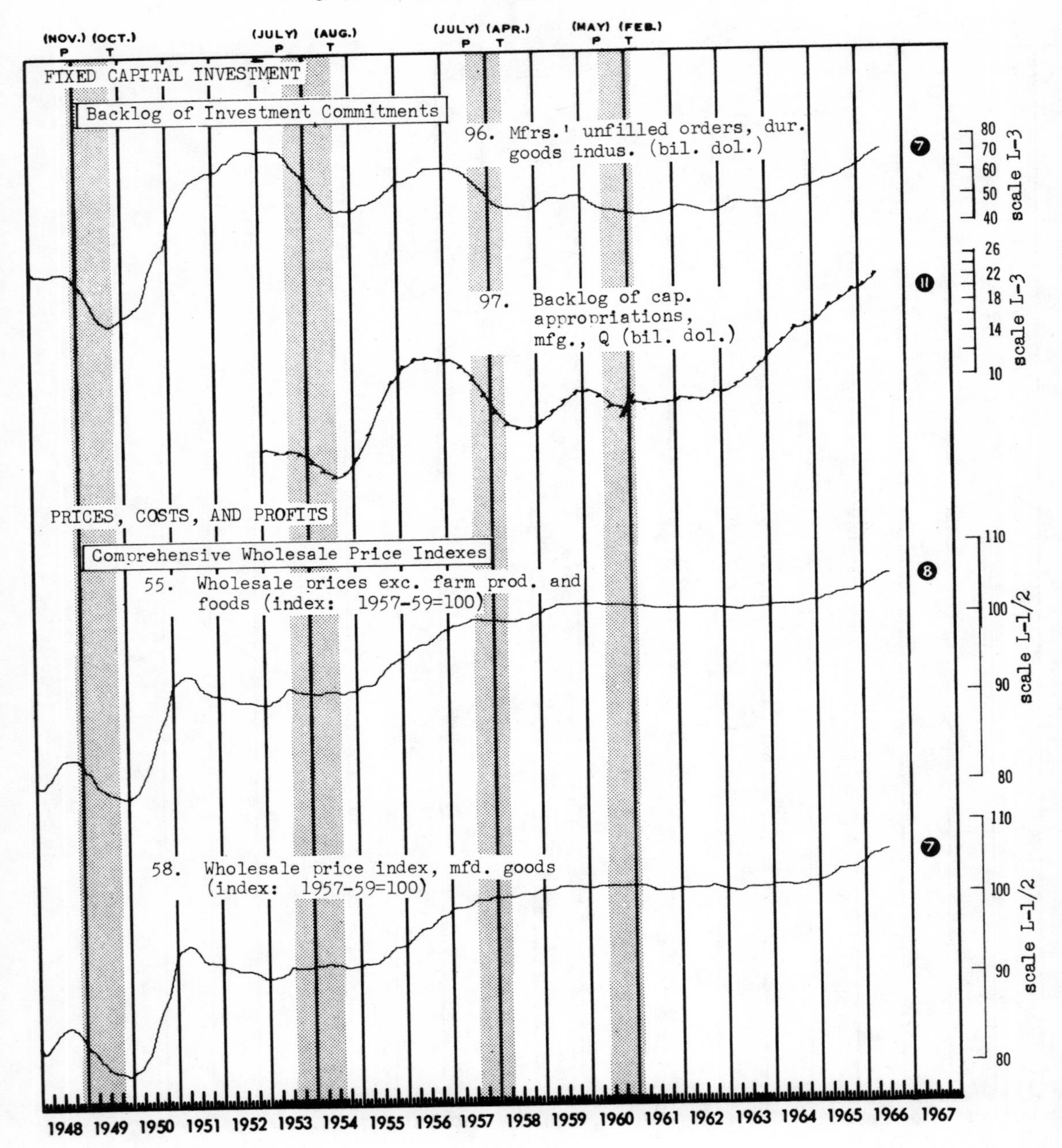

CHART 1

Eighty-eight Selected Indicators Classified by Timing and Economic Process

Roughly Coincident Indicators, 25 Series (Concluded)

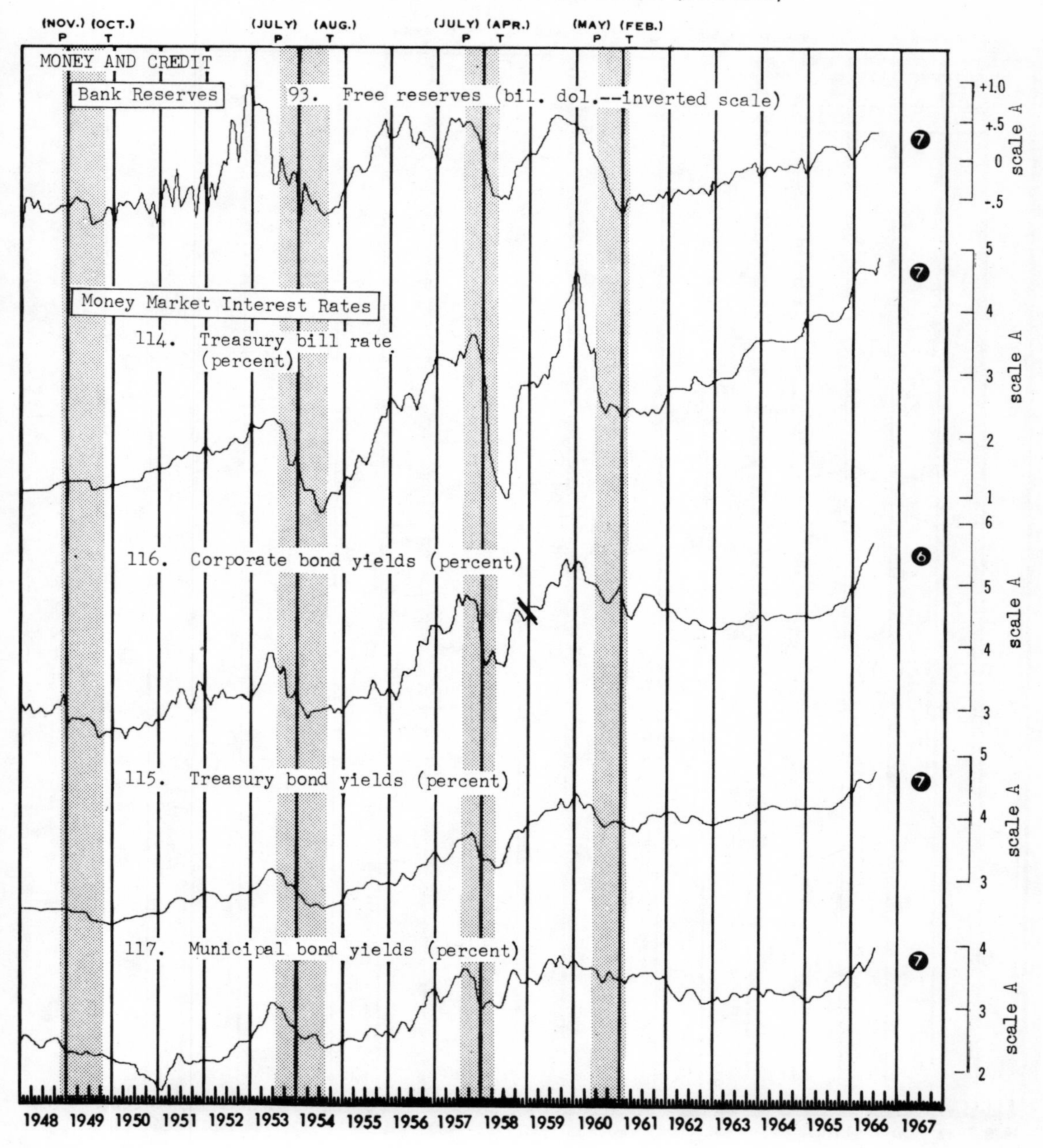

CHART 1

Eighty-eight Selected Indicators Classified by Timing and Economic Process

Lagging Indicators, 11 Series

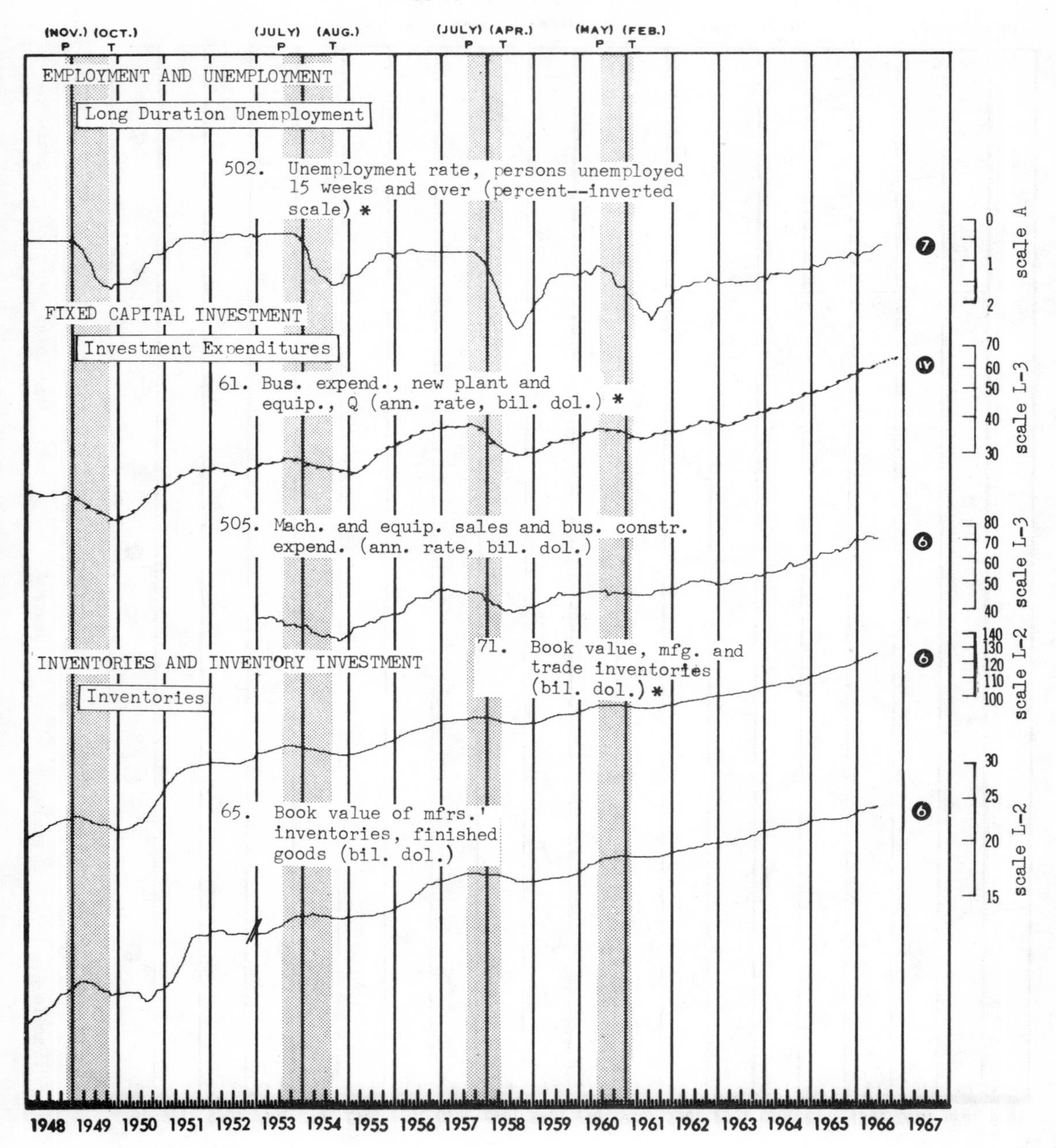

CHART 1

Eighty-eight Selected Indicators Classified by Timing and Economic Process

Lagging Indicators, 11 Series (Concluded)

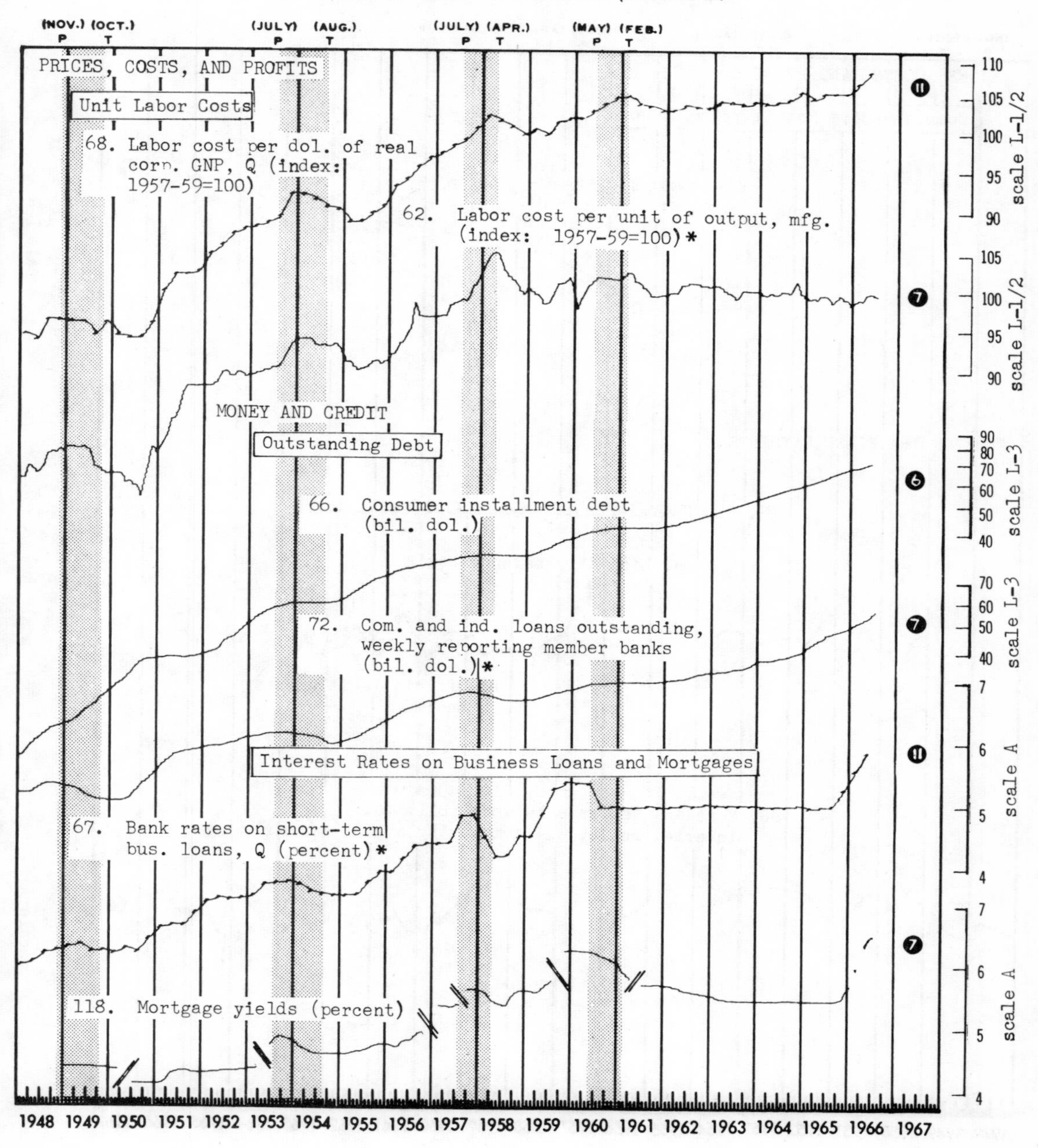

CHART 1

Eighty-eight Selected Indicators Classified by Timing and Economic Process

Other Selected Series, 16 Series

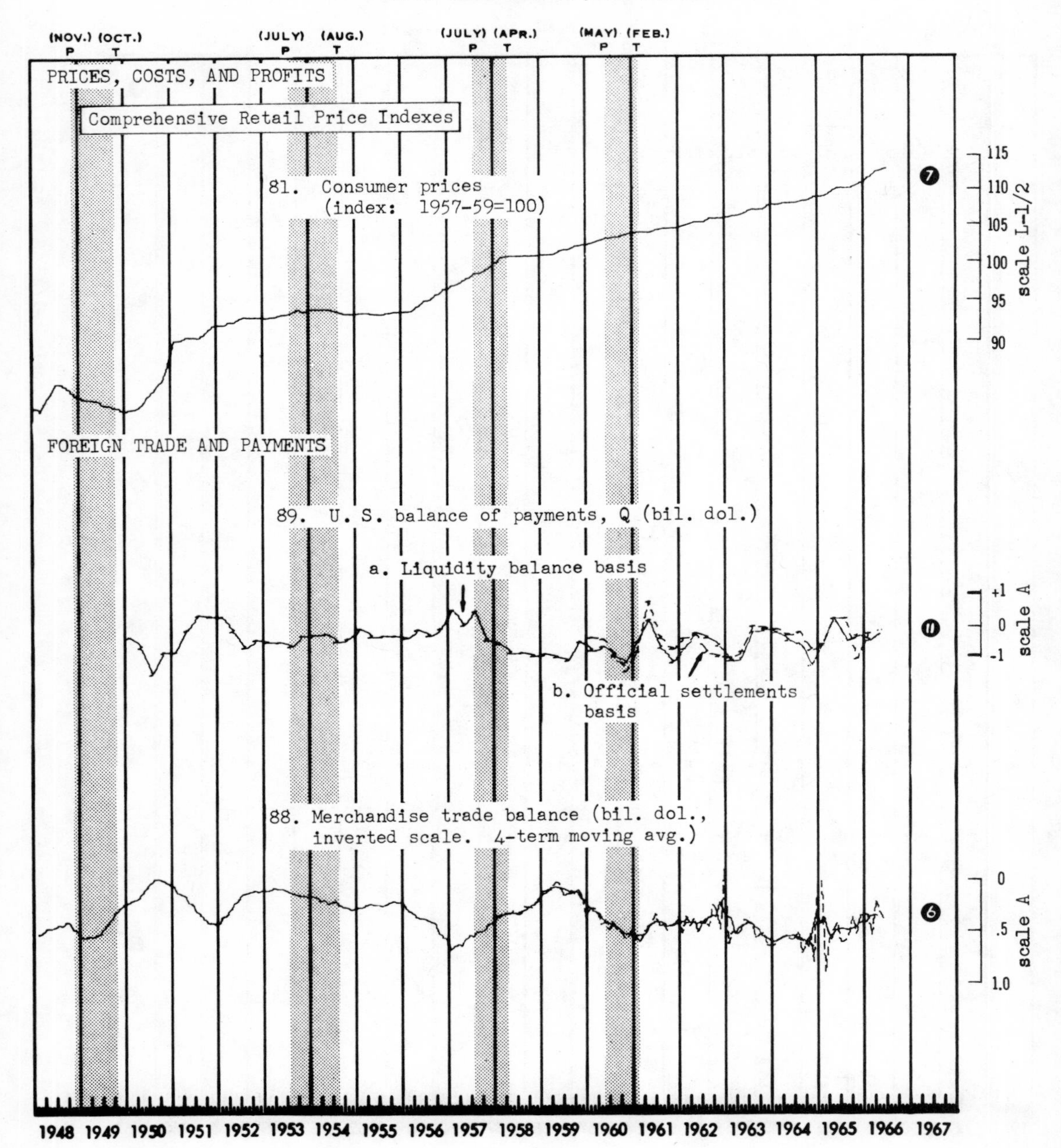

CHART 1

Eighty-eight Selected Indicators Classified by Timing and Economic Process

Other Selected Series, 16 Series (Continued)

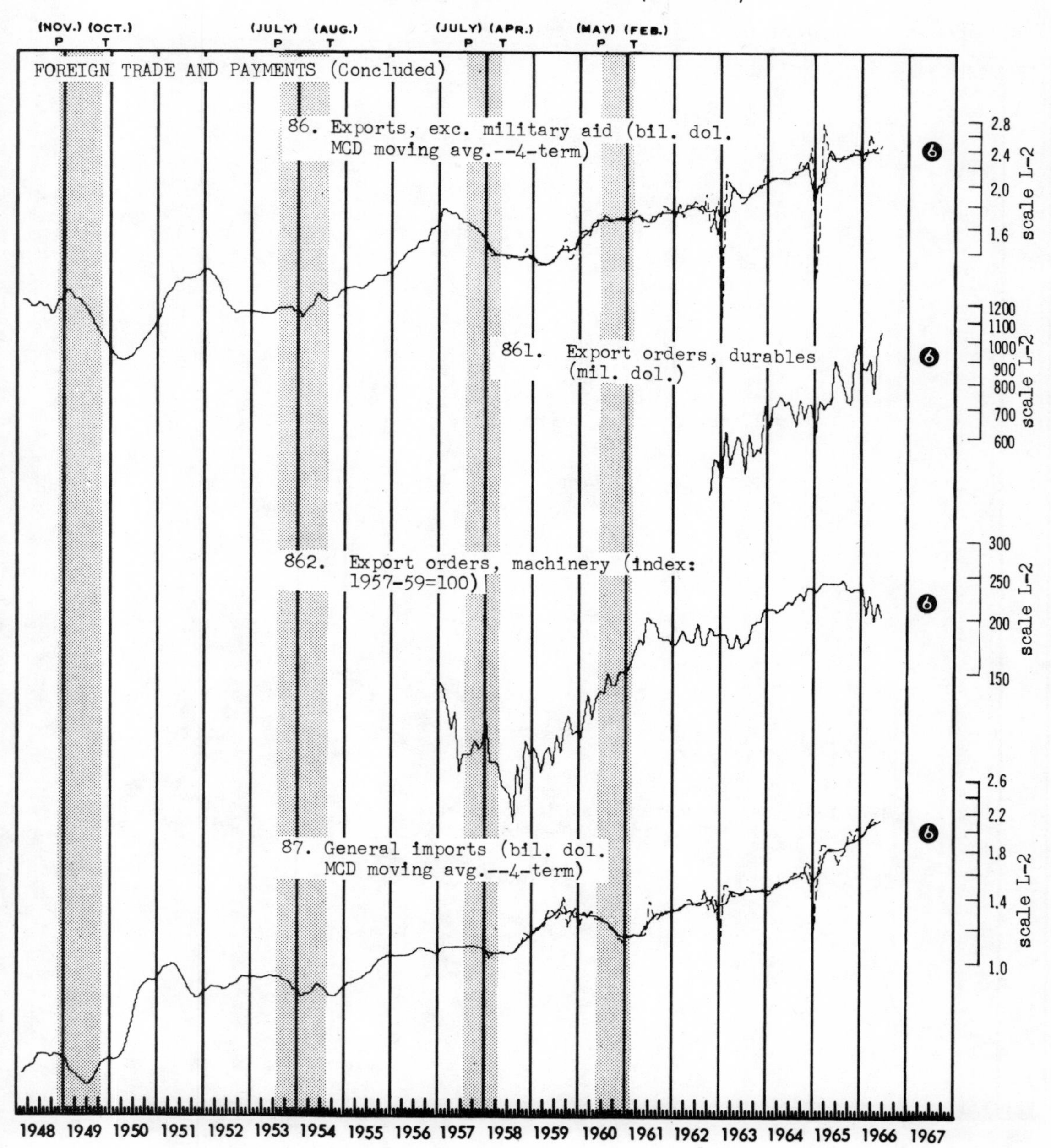

CHART 1

Eighty-eight Selected Indicators Classified by Timing and Economic Process

Other Selected Series, 16 Series (Continued)

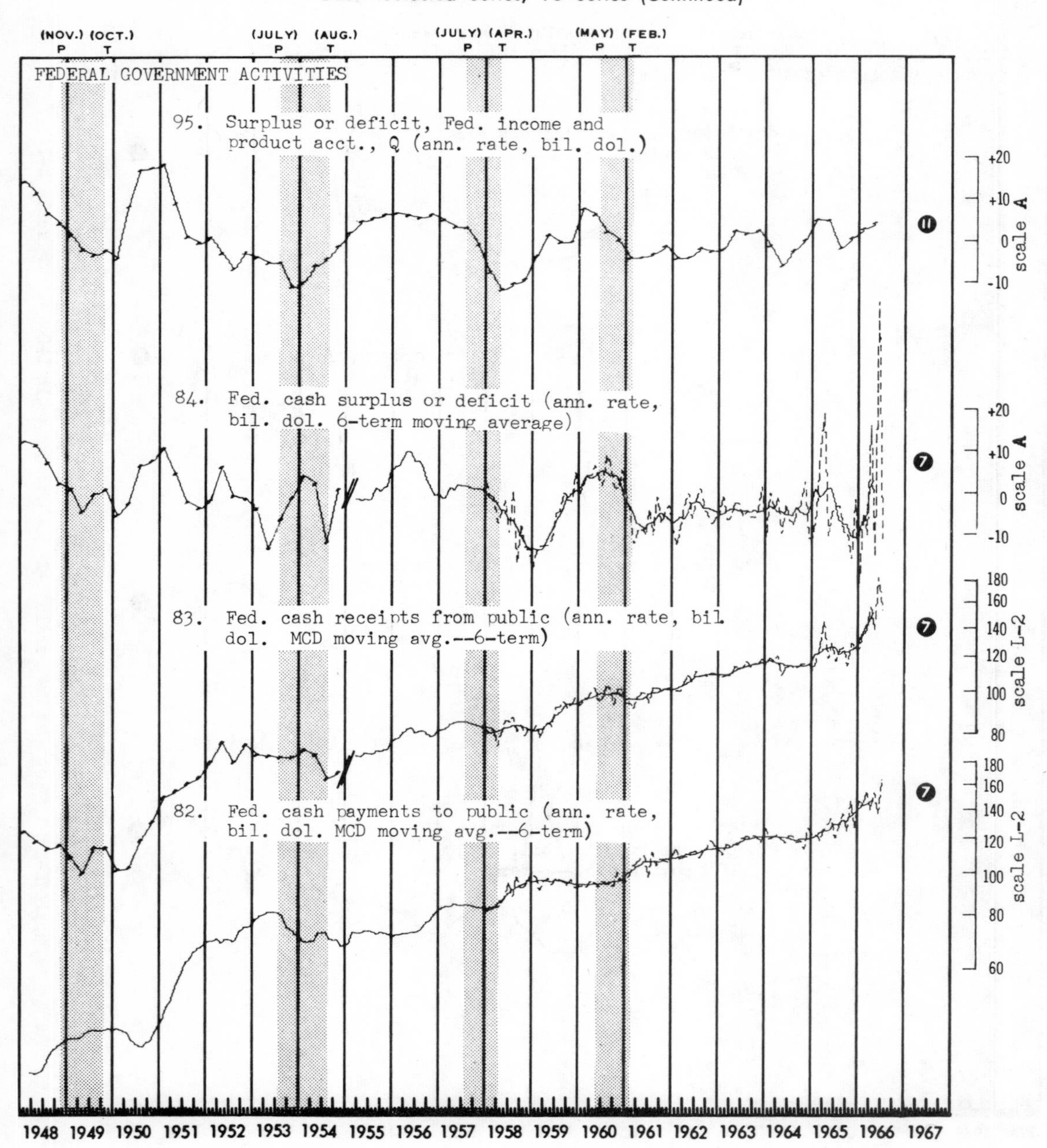

CHART 1

Eighty-eight Selected Indicators Classified by Timing and Economic Process

Other Selected Series, 16 Series (Concluded)

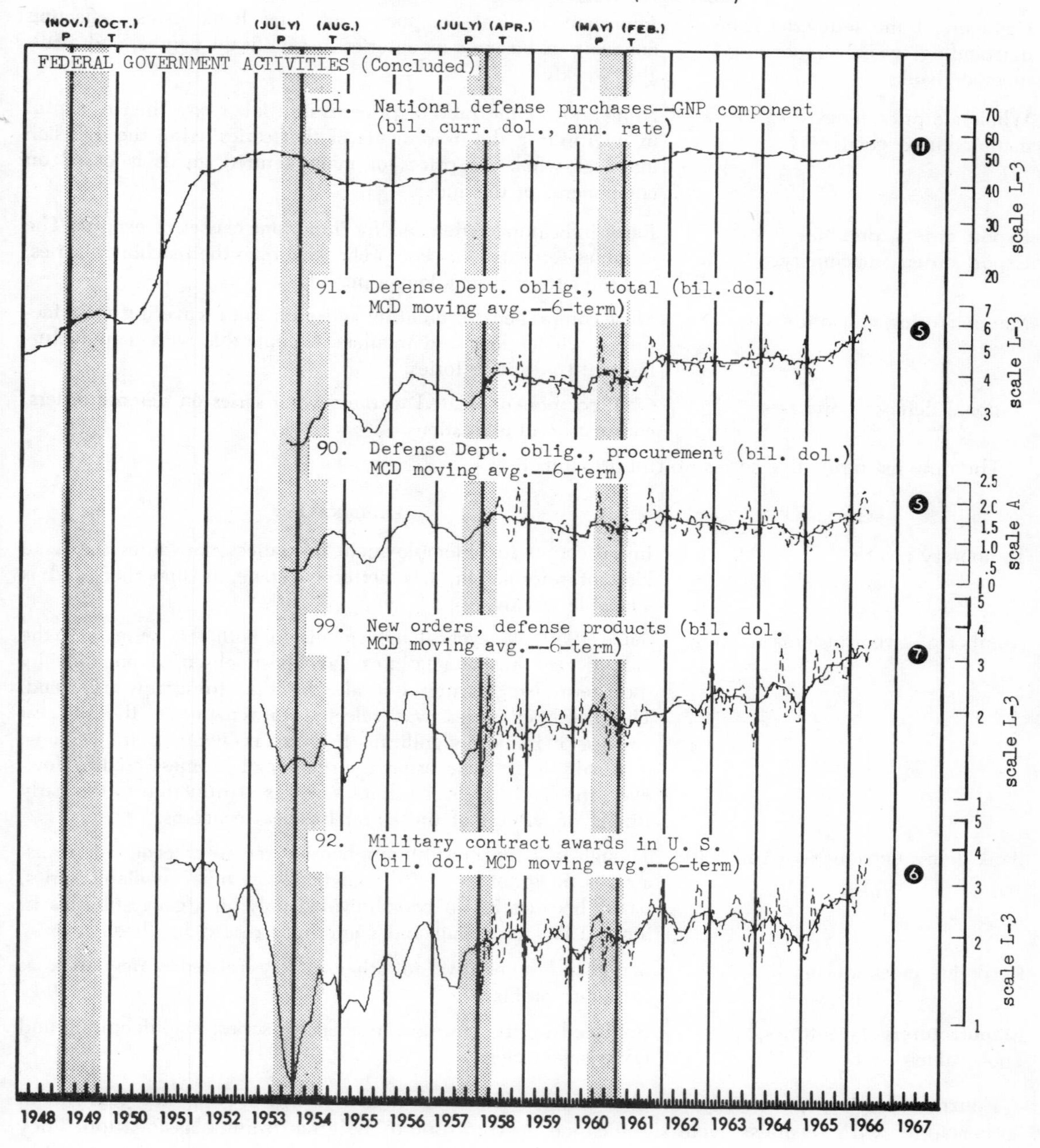

SERIES	EXPLANATION
Book value, manufacturing and trade inventories	Most comprehensive monthly series on inventories.
Commercial and industrial loans outstanding, weekly reporting member banks	Important cyclical component of total bank loans, reflecting financing of business inventories in significant degree, and available weekly.
Wholesale price index, manufactured goods	Numerator of the ratio of price to unit labor cost; hence helpful in interpreting the movements of that series. Also, the diffusion index of wholesale prices of manufactured goods is based on components of this index.
Export orders, durables Export orders, machinery	Early indicators of demand for important classes of exports. The durables series is more comprehensive than the machinery series, but the latter covers a longer period.
Manufacturing and trade sales	Most comprehensive monthly series on sales, covering manufacturers, wholesalers, and retailers. Comparable with manufacturing and trade inventories.
National defense purchases	GNP component related to the several series on defense orders, contracts, and obligations.

The new list omits five series on the previous list:

SERIES	EXPLANATION
Temporary layoffs	Initial claims for unemployment insurance contributes the same kind of information, has better coverage, is smoother, and is available weekly.
Number of large business failures	Since 1950 the cyclical movements in both this series and the liabilities of business failures have been obscured not only by short-term irregularities but also by the strong upward trend. The liabilities series was selected to remain on the full list because it is more significant from an economic point of view, especially in its bearing on the quality of business credit. However, the lead in the liabilities series is attributable to the early timing of failures of the larger business concerns.
Bank debits outside New York City	Though still the most comprehensive record of economic transactions, it is not as useful analytically as other available series, partly because it can be subdivided only on a geographic basis. Since 1950 its timing and conformity record has been poor.
Corporate gross savings	Score is low relative to other closely related series, such as corporate profits.
Manufacturers' inventories, book value	Replaced by the more comprehensive series, manufacturing and trade inventories.

Fourteen series, previously in the group "other series with business cycle significance," have been assigned a timing classification. Most of these series were added in 1963 in order to provide additional information on financial markets, but it was not feasible at that time to assign a timing classification. They are as follows: residential mortgage yields, change in consumer instalment debt, change in bank loans to business, total funds raised, free reserves, change in money supply, change in money supply plus time deposits, Treasury bill rate, yield on long-term U.S. bonds, corporate bond yields, municipal bond yields, total construction contracts, unfilled orders for durable goods, and backlog of capital appropriations. The timing classification of all other series presently shown in *Business Cycle Developments* remains the same.

3. THE SHORT LIST

The short list, identified by asterisks in Table 6 and Chart 1, and listed separately in Table 7, includes 25 U.S. series—12 leading, 7 coincident, and 6 lagging; 21 are monthly and 4 quarterly. All the series on this list have high scores, and they involve very little duplication.

Fourteen series are retained from the 1960 list of 26 indicators and six are substitutes for fairly closely related series on the 1960 list. Five substantially new series are put on the list and six are dropped.[3] Table 8 recapitulates these changes and explains them briefly.

Although the general character of the new short list does not differ substantially from the 1960 list, the improvements are not, we believe, negligible. Whereas on the 1960 list seven of the series were quarterly, the new list includes only four quarterly series. Whereas the 1960 list contained six series pertaining to manufacturing industries alone, the new list includes only four series with such limited coverage. Whereas the 1960 list includes six series with rather low scores for timing or conformity or both, only two series in the new list fail to measure up to the rest in this respect.[4] Further, the new list contains three important series that had not been constructed at the time the 1960 list was compiled: contracts and orders for plant and equipment, ratio of prices to unit labor cost in manufacturing, and index of business formation. Hence the new short list is more promptly available, has broader coverage, has achieved a superior record of performance, and includes several new and improved indicators.

4. THE OTHER SERIES SCORED

Altogether 122 series were covered in the present review, with 88 placed on the full list of indicators and 34 excluded. The scores and timing classifications of the excluded series are shown in Table 9 and the series are plotted in Chart 2. These series fall primarily into two groups. First, series with good records and high scores were excluded because they did not seem to contribute sufficiently to warrant displacing other series or increasing the length of the list. Examples are gross national product as estimated from the income side of the accounts (score: 75), steel ingot production (67), and employment in commodity-producing industries (78). Such series are unquestionably valuable in their own right for purposes of business cycle analysis. The other group is made up of series with relatively low scores, which indicate that they have certain limitations as cyclical indicators. Examples are employment in the service industries (47), personal consumption expendi-

[3] Five of the six series dropped from the short list are retained on the full list. The exception, bank debits outside New York City, is explained above. Note, however, that the latter's geographic breakdown makes it valuable as a regional or local indicator.

[4] The six series on the 1960 list with low scores are liabilities of business failures (which has a good record over its long history but not since 1948); contracts for commercial and industrial construction; bank debits outside New York; wholesale price index, excluding farm products and foods; sales of retail stores; and consumer instalment debt outstanding. The two low-scoring series on the new list are sales of retail stores, retained because of its broad significance; and commercial and industrial loans outstanding, with a record marred largely by its failure to register a cyclical contraction during the mild 1960–61 recession.

TABLE 7
Short List of Indicators: Scores and Timing Characteristics

			Scores, Six Criteria						Timing at Peaks and Tro			
Classification and Series Title (1)	First Business Cycle Turn Covered (2)	Average Score (3)	Economic Significance (4)	Statistical Adequacy (5)	Conformity (6)	Timing (7)	Smoothness (8)	Currency (9)	Business Cycle Turns Covered (10)	Leads (11)	Rough Coincidences[a] (12)	Lags (13)
Leading indicators (12 series)												
1. Avg. workweek, prod. workers, mfg.	1921	66	50	65	81	66	60	80	19	13	4(2)	2
30. Nonagri. placements, BES	1945	68	75	63	63	58	80	80	10	8	4(0)	1
38. Index of net business formation	1945	68	75	58	81	67	80	40	10	8	3(1)	0
6. New orders, dur. goods indus.	1920	78	75	72	88	84	60	80	20	16	7(1)	0
10. Contracts and orders, plant and equipment	1948	64	75	63	92	50	40	40	8	7	2(0)	1
29. New building permits, private housing units	1918	67	50	60	76	80	60	80	22	17	5(1)	1
31. Change in book value, mfg. and trade inventories	1945	65	75	67	77	78	20	40	10	9	2(1)	0
23. Industrial materials prices	1919	67	50	72	79	44	80	100	21	13	9(4)	2
19. Stock prices, 500 common stocks	1873	81	75	74	77	87	80	100	44	33	14(2)	5
16. Corporate profits after taxes, Q	1920	68	75	70	79	76	60	25	20	13	11(4)	2
17. Ratio, price to unit labor cost, mfg.	1919	69	50	67	84	72	60	80	21	17	10(1)	3
113. Change in consumer instalment debt	1929	63	50	79	77	60	60	40	14	11	4(0)	1
Roughly coincident indicators (7 series)												
41. Employees in nonagri. establishments	1929	81	75	61	90	87	100	80	14	6	12(6)	2
43. Unemployment rate, total (inv.)	1929	75	75	63	96	60	80	80	14	4	8(3)	6
50. GNP in constant dollars, expenditure estimate, Q	1921	73	75	75	91	58	80	50	17	7	9(3)	3
47. Industrial production	1919	72	75	63	94	38	100	80	21	9	13(9)	3
52. Personal income	1921	74	75	73	89	43	100	80	19	10	12(2)	5
816. Mfg. and trade sales	1948	71	75	68	70	80	80	40	8	4	6(4)	0
54. Sales of retail stores	1919	69	75	77	89	12	80	100	21	5	7(1)	6
Lagging indicators (6 series)												
502. Unempl. rate, persons unempl. 15+ weeks (inv.)	1948	69	50	63	98	52	80	80	8	1	5(1)	6
61. Bus. expend., plant and equip., Q	1918	86	75	77	96	94	100	80	20	2	16(5)	13
71. Book value, mfg. and trade inventories	1945	71	75	67	75	66	100	40	10	2	7(0)	8
62. Labor cost per unit of output, mfg.	1919	68	50	70	83	56	80	80	21	0	1(0)	14
72. Comm. and indus. loans outstanding	1937	57	50	47	67	20	100	100	12	1	6(0)	7
67. Bank rates, short-term bus. loans, Q	1919	60	50	55	82	47	80	50	21	2	5(1)	15

[a] Rough coincidences include exact coincidences (shown in parentheses) and leads and lags of 3 months or less. Leads (lags) include leads month or more. The total number of timing comparisons, which can be less than the number of business cycle turns covered by the series, is the s leads, exact coincidences, and lags. Leads and lags of quarterly series are expressed in terms of months.

TABLE 8
Relation Between the 1966 and the 1960 Short Lists of Indicators

1966 List	1960 List	Reason for Change
Leading series		
Average workweek, mfg.	Same	
New orders, dur. goods	Same	
Indus. mater. price index	Same	
Stock price index	Same	
Corp. profits after taxes, Q	Same	
Nonagri. placements	Accession rate, mfg.	Placements provide broader coverage and prompter availability
Index of bus. formation	Net change in bus. pop., Q	Net change series discontinued
New bldg. permits, housing	Housing starts	Permits series is smoother
Change in book value, mfg. and trade inventories	Change in business inventories, Q	Monthly series more current
Contracts and orders, plant and equipment		Most comprehensive series on new investment commitments by business enterprises; new since 1960 list
Ratio, price to unit labor cost, mfg.		Best available monthly index of profit margins; new since 1960 list
Change in consumer instal. debt		Wide cyclical movements and consistent leads; replaces consumer debt outstanding
	Layoff rate, mfg.	Workweek and placements enough for short list
	Liabilities of bus. failures	Poor timing and conformity record since 1948
	Constr. contracts, comm. and indus., floor space	Poor timing and conformity record since 1950. The equivalent value series, plus privately owned public utilities, is included in the series on contracts and orders
Roughly coincident series		
Nonagri. employment	Same	
Unemployment rate, total	Same	
GNP in constant $, Q	Same	
Industrial production	Same	
Personal income	Same	
Sales of retail stores	Same	
Mfg. and trade sales		Most comprehensive monthly series on sales, comparable with mfg. and trade inventories
	GNP in current $, Q	Constant $ GNP sufficient for short list, especially in view of inclusion of current $ series on mfg. and trade sales
	Bank debits outside N.Y.C.	Poor timing and conformity record since 1950
	Wholesale price index, excl. farm products and foods	Poor timing and conformity record since 1950
Lagging series		
Plant and equip. expend., Q	Same	
Unit labor cost, mfg.	Same	
Bank rates on bus. loans, Q	Same	
Book value, mfg. and trade inventories	Book value, mfg. inventories	Most comprehensive monthly series on inventories
Comm. and indus. loans outstanding	Consumer instalment debt	More cyclically sensitive than consumer debt; net change in consumer debt included in leading group
Unemploy. rate, 15+ weeks		Represents longer duration and hence more serious unemployment

tures for durable goods (51), and new orders for machine tools (59).

It must be emphasized that these series may be helpful in other important uses, for example, in industry studies or studies of long-term economic growth. They are also of value in business cycle analysis, else they would not have been reviewed at all. Series on particular industries or occupations help to identify areas of strength and of weakness, and contribute to an understanding of recent trends and prospects. Similarly, series that distinguish employment in the relatively stable service industries from the more cyclical commodity-producing industries are useful in assessing the effect on the business cycle of the far more rapid secular growth in the service industries.

The distinction between the series in this excluded group that have relatively low scores and series included in the full list but unclassified by timing is not clearly defined. The scoring plan does not help much here, since both groups generally have low scores. Inclusion or exclusion of these series is primarily a matter of judgment as to the degree of interest attaching to particular series. Furthermore, we have undoubtedly given this matter less attention than it warrants, and some series that are important in assessing short-run business prospects, despite weaknesses as business indicators, do not appear in either the excluded or the included (unclassified) group. Examples that come to mind are series on hourly earnings, output per man-hour, labor force, and capital stock or industrial capacity. Further study should be devoted to this matter in later work, with a view to improving and perhaps enlarging the "unclassified" group.

5. THE ROLE OF QUANTITATIVE STANDARDS

In setting up the classification scheme and the final selection of indicators, it became evident that the scoring plan could not be used mechanically, for several reasons.

First, the rules for designating the timing classification of the individual series did not always yield sensible results. In some instances the behavior of the series since 1948 did not support the classification based on the entire period, and the evidence of the shorter but more recent period had to be weighed against that of the longer period. In other instances closely related series were inconsistently classified by the mechanical rules, because the series covered different periods or experienced different irregular fluctuations. Most of these inconsistencies were of small moment, and it seemed unwise either to emphasize or to perpetuate them in a classification. Hence we decided to determine the appropriate timing classification for each of the minor economic groups of series in Table 6, column 1, basing the decision on the evidence provided by the series in the group. In this way, the evidence for closely related series could be brought to bear on the classification of individual series, and in most cases this seemed to yield sensible results. Hence the final timing classification for a series is the same as that for the group within which it is placed. The instances where this conflicts with the application of the mechanical rules for classifying individual series are indicated in the table.[5]

A second type of deviation from a mechanical application of the scoring plan in selecting indicators was occasioned by the advantage of including two closely related series even though one had a substantially lower score than the other. For example, new capital appropriations of manufacturing industries is included despite its lower score than contracts and orders for plant and equipment; profits per dollar of sales in manufacturing is included despite its lower score than the ratio of prices to unit labor costs. The merits of one series compensate for some of the limitations

[5] The group classification procedure has not been extended to the separate classifications of peak and trough timing shown in Appendixes B and C. There the classification is based simply on the mechanical rules.

of the other. On the other hand, an effort was made to eliminate duplication where no important purpose appeared to be served by it. It also seemed desirable to restrict the proportion of series pertaining to manufacturing alone, and to restrict the number of series that were components of or aggregates derived from series included. Examples of series with high scores omitted for these reasons are manufacturers' inventories and nonagricultural employment in commodity-producing industries. Finally, as mentioned above, the scoring plan was not especially helpful in aiding decisions on series in the group unclassified by cyclical timing.

In making up the short list, several additional factors were taken into account:

1. A very low score for one of the six scoring categories was considered sufficient reason for deciding against a series when two related series with very close total scores were being considered. For this reason, e.g., housing permits was selected over housing starts.

2. Series with uncertain timing or conformity were rejected. This uncertainty may take the form of leads which are equal to or longer than the corresponding business cycle phases (a lead at troughs which starts before the preceding business cycle peak has been reached) or which cross opposite specific turns. The uncertainty may also pertain to whether timing comparisons should be made positively or invertedly. The series on the rate of change in the money supply provides an example of such uncertainty on both counts (cf. Chapter II, note 9).

3. The score for the period since 1948 was weighed more heavily. Thus, the wholesale price index was excluded from the short list because of its poor timing record in the four most recent business cycles.

Some or all of these additional criteria might, indeed, have been taken into account in setting up the scoring plan. Thus, although the present scoring plan enlarges the role of quantitative criteria in selecting indicators, it does not go as far as may be possible. It is a further, but not the ultimate, extension of the role of quantitative standards that have been used in making the selections of NBER indicators over the years.

Average scores for various groups of series are provided in Table 10. It is interesting to observe that the series on the short list (line 2) have the highest final score on the average (70), and that the averages for the short list exceed those for the full list in each of the six categories. The series on the full list unclassified by timing (line 1d) have the lowest average score (47). The series scored but omitted from the final list (line 3) have a fairly high average score, but, as noted, many high-scoring series were omitted for special reasons stated above.

These results are no accident since the scores and the information on which they were based were used in selecting the series. It is evident, however, from our previous discussion that we did not follow the scores mechanically in selecting series. The averages show that we did not ignore them either.

The table also shows that the leading indicators are the most erratic and the lagging indicators the smoothest. The coincident indicators have the shortest publication lag. The coincident indicators also have the highest conformity scores, an expected result since the NBER business cycle chronology is largely based on these series. The statistical adequacy scores for each group are about the same on the average.

6. THE CONTRIBUTION OF THE NEW LIST

The question is often—and properly—raised as to how useful the business cycle indicators are in making short-term forecasts. This question has been dealt with in previous publications of the National Bureau as well as in articles prepared by others, and we shall not

TABLE 9
Thirty-four Other Series Classified by Economic Process: Scores and Timing Characteristics

Economic Process and Series Title	First Business Cycle Turn Covered	Average Score	Scores, Six Criteria: Economic Significance	Statistical Adequacy	Conformity	Timing	Smoothness	Currency	Timing at Peaks and Troughs: Business Cycle Turns Covered	Leads	Rough Coincidences[a]	Lags	Median Lead(−) or Lag(+) in Months
(1)	(2)	(3)	(4)	(5)	(6)	(7)	(8)	(9)	(10)	(11)	(12)	(13)	(14)
1. Employment and unemployment													
Marginal employment adjustments													
805. Accession rate, new hires, mfg.	1953	57	50	66	66	42	80	40	6	5	2(1)	0	−6
806. Accession rate, rehires, mfg. (inv.)[b]	1953	56	50	66	57	68	40	40	6	3	3(0)	3	0
4. No. of persons on temporary layoff (inv.)	1948	62	75	63	98	24	20	80	8	5	3(2)	0	−9
Job vacancies													
809. Help-wanted display ads, exec. positions	1954	52	50	30	54	56	60	80	5	5	1(0)	0	−5
Employment													
801. Man-hours, nonagri. employees, persons with a job	1945	68	75	62	81	50	60	80	10	6	4(1)	1	−4
802. Man-hours, nonagri. employees, persons at work	1945	68	75	65	81	48	60	80	10	6	4(1)	1	−2
807. Nonagri. empl., commodity-prod. indus.	1945	78	75	60	89	78	100	80	10	5	6(3)	2	−2
808. Nonagri. empl., service indus.	1945	47	50	60	20	16	100	80	10	1	5(1)	4	+1
Unemployment													
803. Unemployment rate, under 5 weeks (inv.)	1948	62	50	63	72	66	40	80	8	6	5(2)	0	−2
804. Unemployment rate, 5–14 weeks (inv.)	1948	62	50	63	73	52	60	80	8	5	5(0)	3	−1
2. Production, income, consumption, and trade													
Production													
810. GNP in current $, income estimate, Q	1945	74	75	70	91	70	100	25	10	3	9(3)	4	0
811. GNP in constant $, income estimate, Q	1948	75	75	68	88	90	80	25	8	2	8(3)	3	0
814. Steel ingot production	1899	67	50	82	96	38	40	100	32	18	17(7)	7	−1
813. Auto production, passenger cars	1913	58	50	82	77	11	40	100	22	8	9(3)	7	0
Consumption and trade													

56. Wholesale sales, merchant wholesalers	1919	66	50	77	84	59	80	40	18	11	10(3)	2	−2
815. Index of truck tonnage hauled	1948	61	50	58	50	78	80	60	8	7	4(1)	0	−4
817. Personal consumption expend., dur. goods, Q	1945	51	50	70	44	27	80	50	10	5	5(2)	1	−2
3. Fixed capital investment													
New investment commitments													
825. New orders, machine tools	1945	59	50	73	89	44	40	40	9	7	2(0)	1	−8
Investment expenditures													
819. Gross priv. dom. investment, total, Q	1945	63	75	70	70	34	80	50	10	7	6(1)	2	−3
818. Gross priv. dom. investment, bus. sec., Q	1945	65	75	70	72	44	80	50	10	1	7(3)	4	0
821. Mfrs.' sales, prod. dur. equip., value	1948	63	50	61	92	51	80	40	8	2	6(0)	6	+2
820. Index of equipment production	1948	70	50	58	92	59	100	80	8	2	7(2)	4	0
822. New construction expend., bus. sec.	1945	42	50	62	4	24	100	40	10	2	4(1)	5	+2
4. Inventories and inventory investment													
Inventories													
64. Mfrs.' inventories, total, value	1926	73	50	73	92	80	100	40	16	3	9(0)	13	+3
Inventory investment and purchasing													
826. Change in stocks on hand and on order, dept. stores	1945	53	50	60	72	62	0	40	10	8	2(0)	0	−10
6. Money and credit													
Flows of money and credit													
827. New nonfarm mortgages recorded, $20,000 and under	1945	40	50	65	44	9	60	0	10	6	0(0)	0	−10
111. Corporate gross savings, Q	1953	45	75	67	29	26	60	0	6	4	4(1)	1	−2
824. Stock offerings, mfg. corp., Q	1953	36	50	71	15	42	0	0	6	4	3(1)	1	−4
823. Stocks, shares sold, N.Y.S.E.	1879	66	50	85	70	65	20	100	43	32	8(2)	5	−7
Credit difficulties													
15. No. of bus. failures, liab. $100,000 and over (inv.)	1894	63	50	74	86	67	0	80	35	25	10(2)	7	−6
828. Delinquency rate, auto direct loans (inv.)	1948	59	50	73	72	48	60	40	8	6	4(0)	2	−4

[a] Rough coincidences include exact coincidences (shown in parentheses) and leads and lags of 3 months or less. Leads (lags) include leads (lags) of 1 month or more. The total number of timing comparisons, which can be less than the number of business cycle turns covered by the series, is the sum of the leads, exact coincidences, and lags. Leads and lags of quarterly series are expressed in terms of months.

[b] Also analyzed positively, in which case the series is classed as leading.

[c] Earlier segment omitted, 1879–1918 (bank clearings).

CHART 2

Thirty-four Other Series Classified by Economic Process

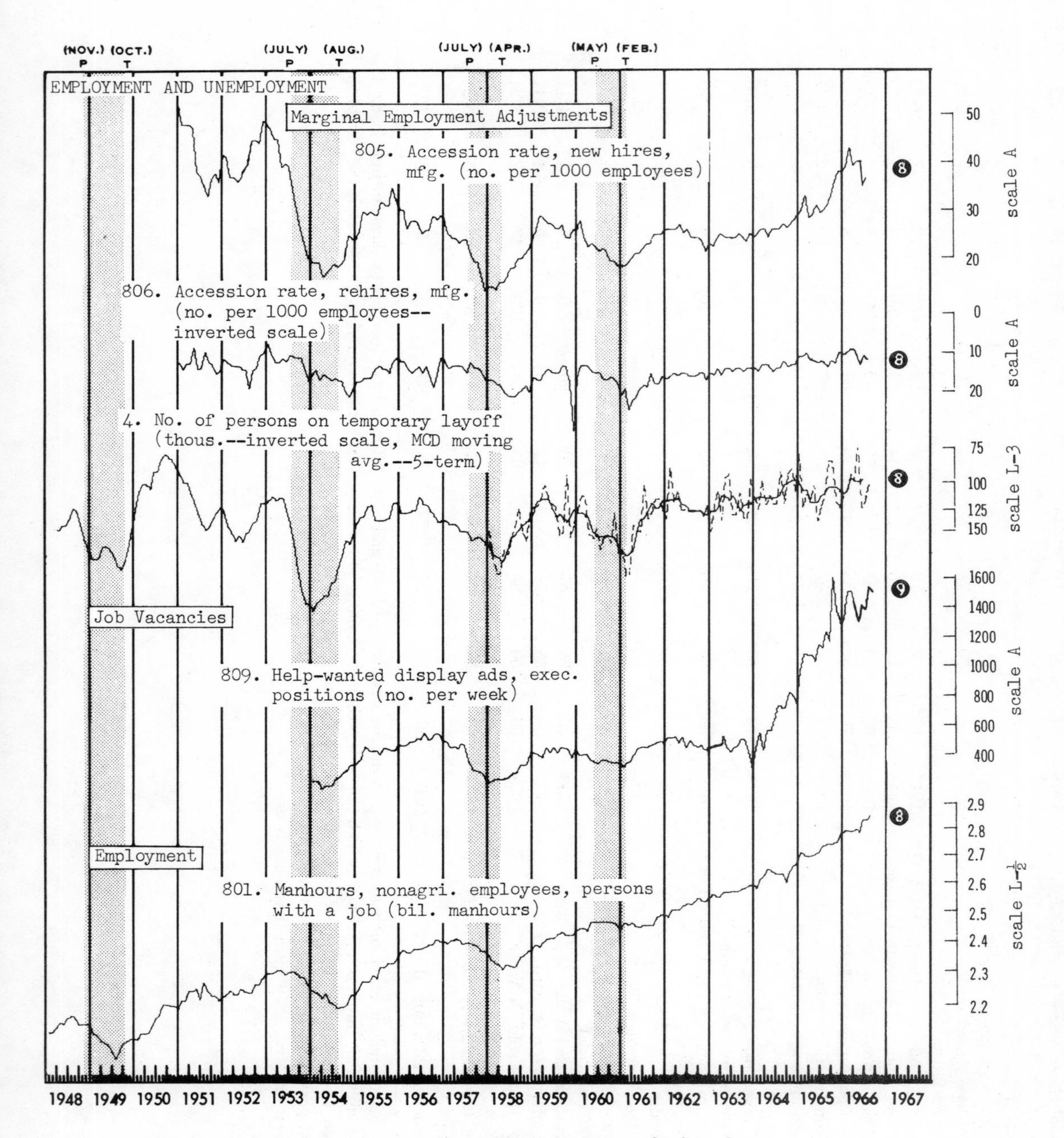

Note: Numbers in the dark circles indicate latest month plotted.

CHART 2

Thirty-four Other Series Classified by Economic Process (Continued)

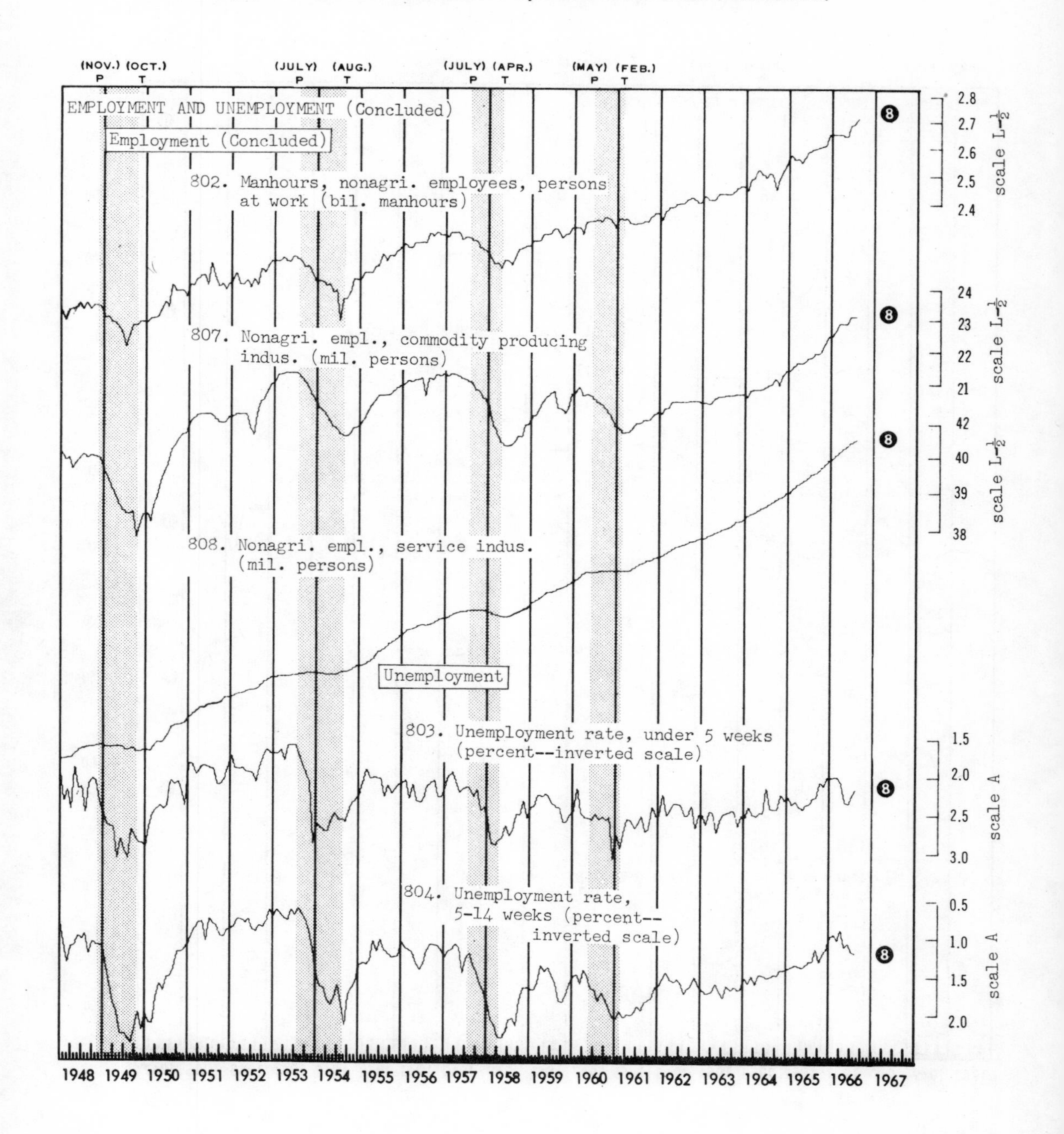

CHART 2

Thirty-four Other Series Classified by Economic Process (Continued)

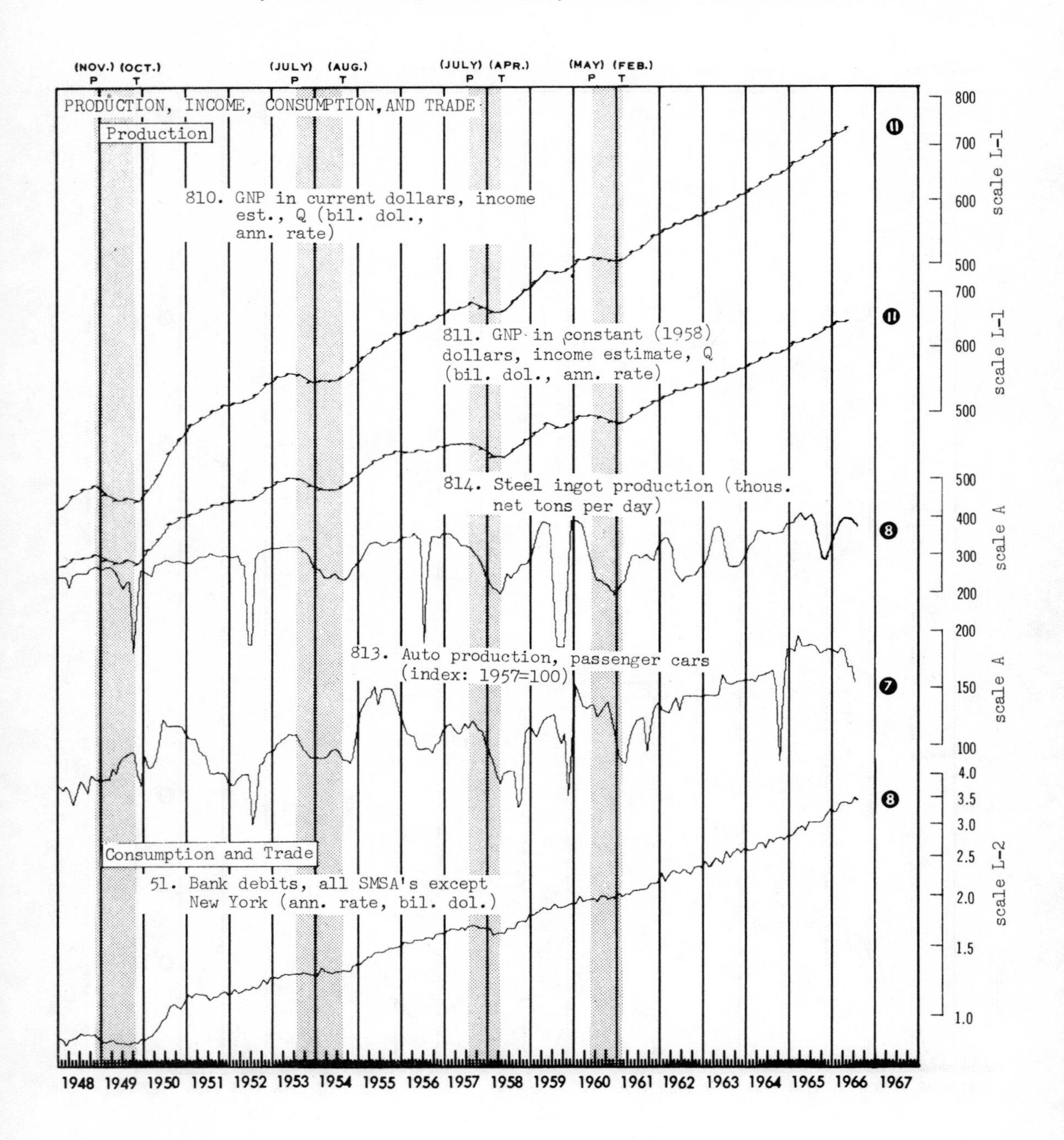

CHART 2

Thirty-four Other Series Classified by Economic Process (Continued)

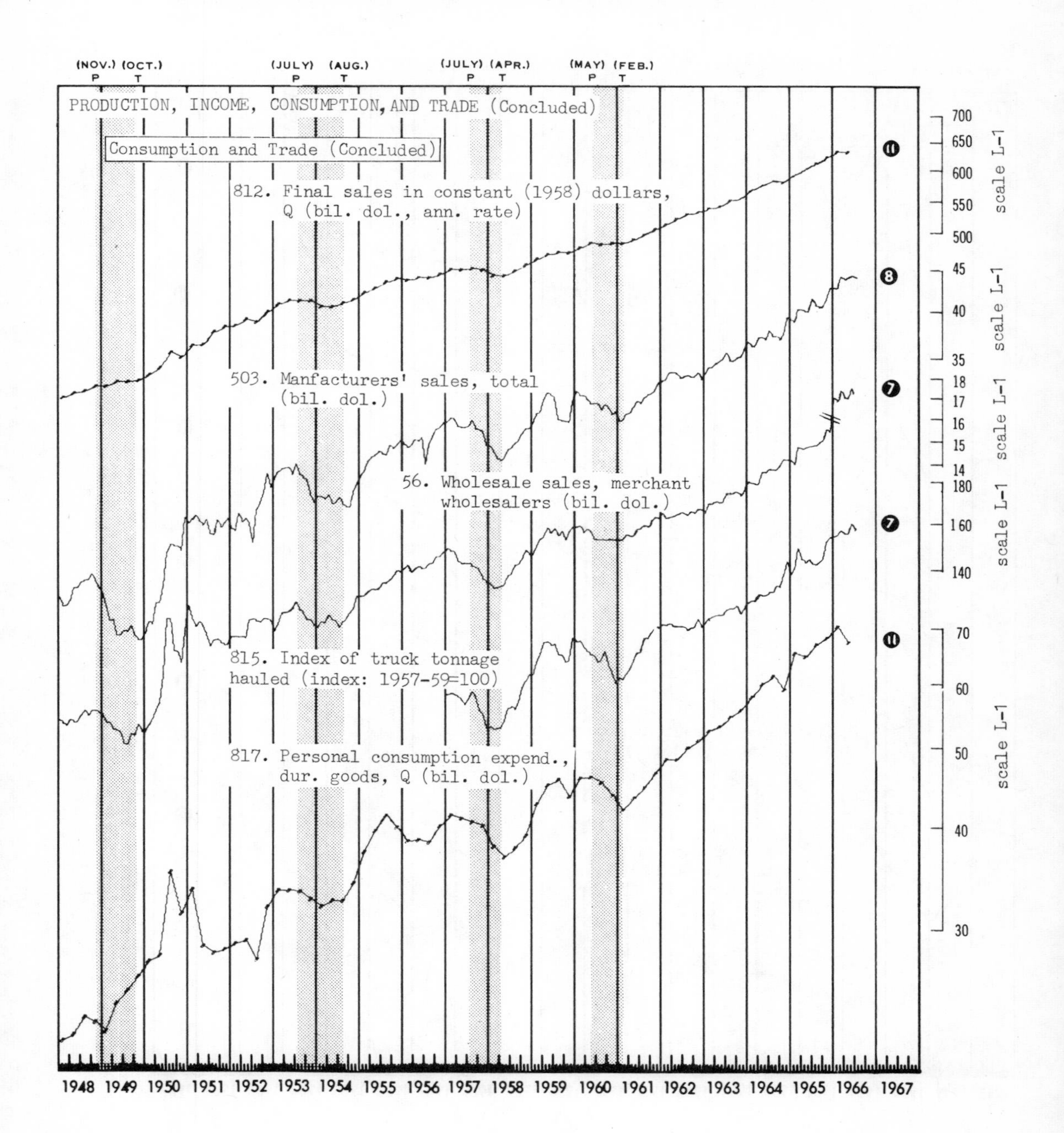

CHART 2

Thirty-four Other Series Classified by Economic Process (Continued)

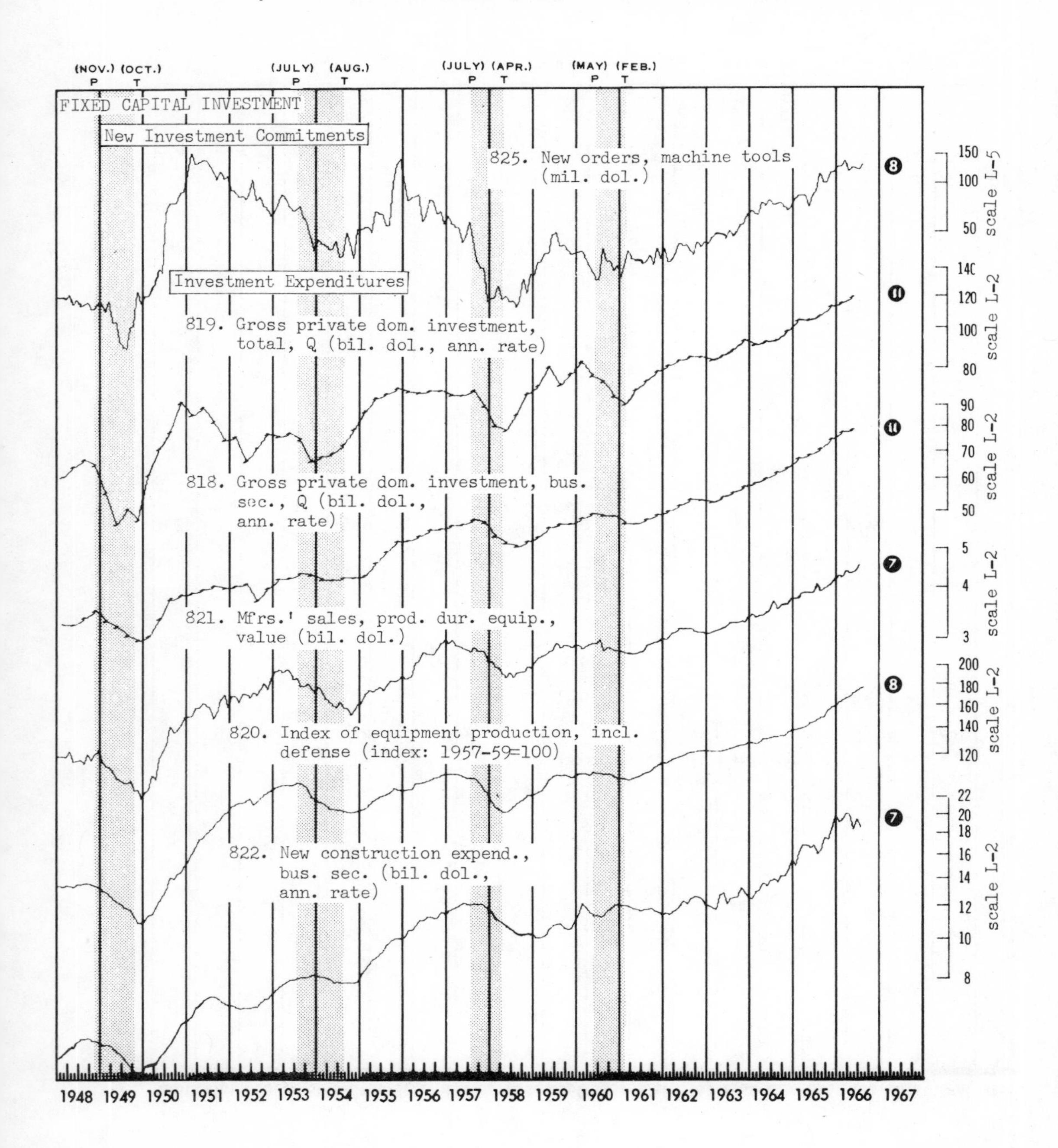

CHART 2

Thirty-four Other Series Classified by Economic Process (Continued)

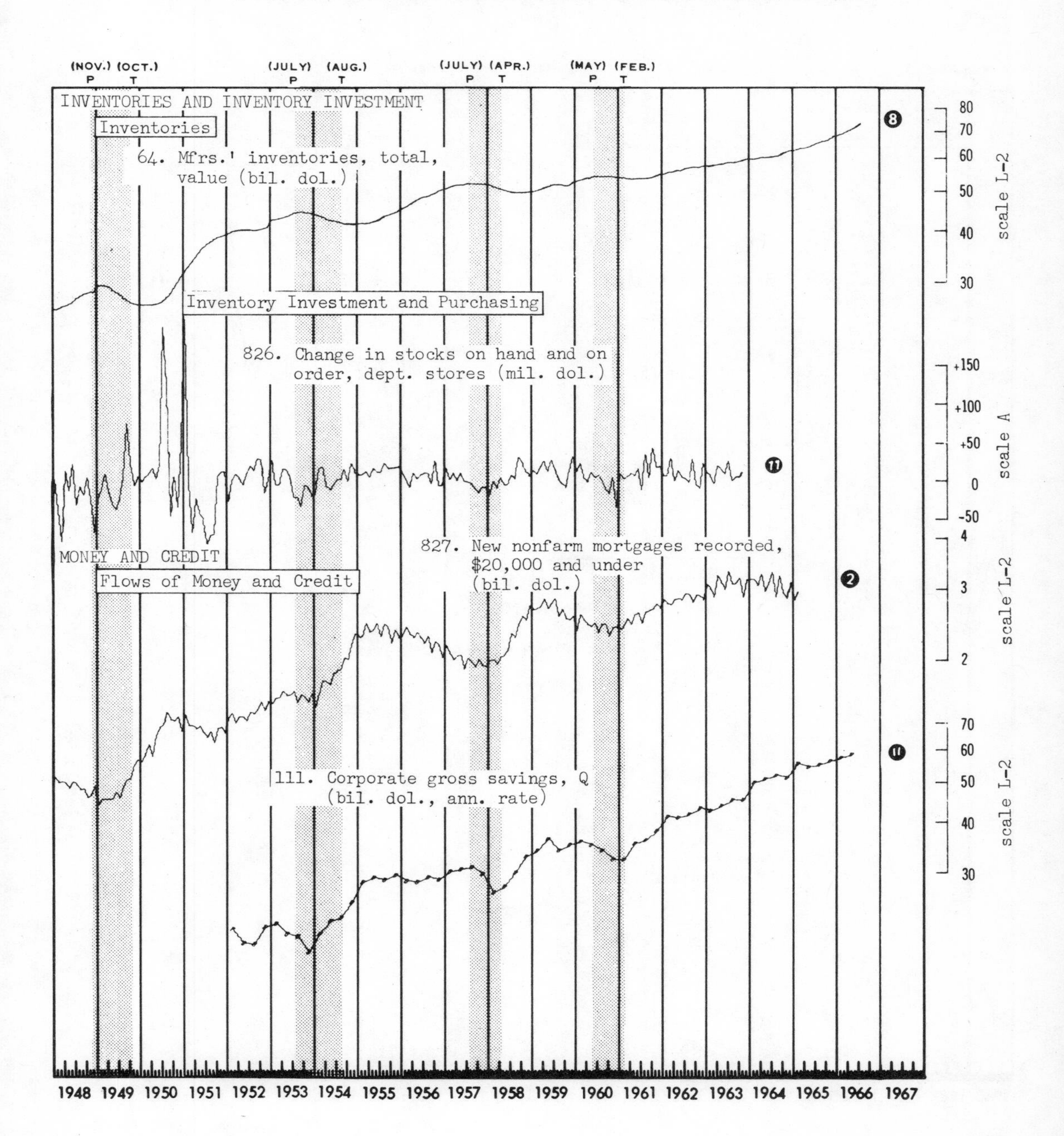

CHART 2

Thirty-four Other Series Classified by Economic Process (Concluded)

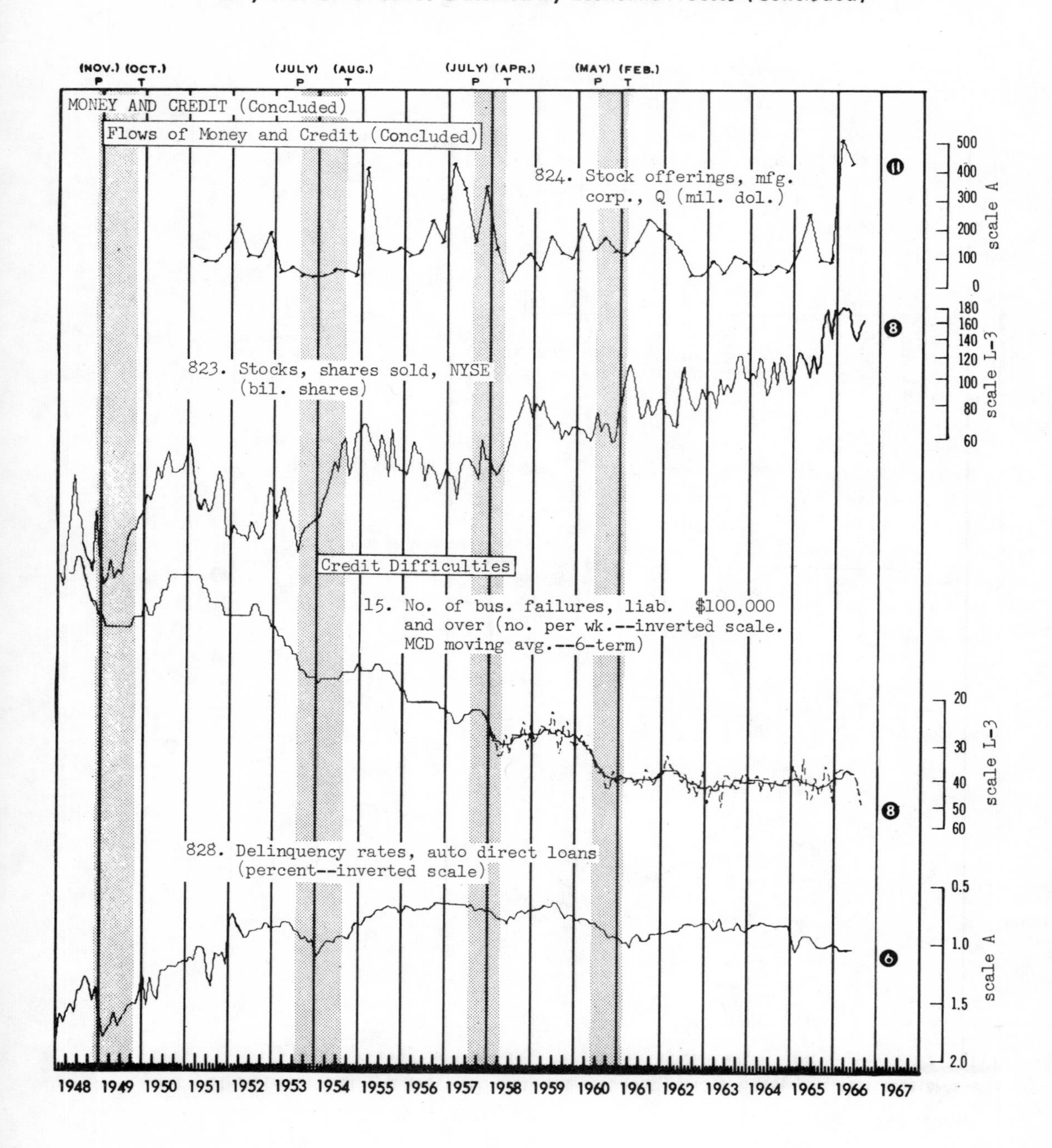

TABLE 10
Average Scores for Selected Groups of Indicators

	All Criteria[a]	Economic Significance	Statistical Adequacy	Conformity	Timing	Smoothness	Currency
1. Full list (86 series)[b]	63	63	65	73	49	62	63
a. Leading (36 series)	64	61	67	75	61	47	59
b. Coincident (25 series)	69	67	66	82	45	87	77
c. Lagging (11 series)	65	59	62	77	52	91	60
d. Unclassified (14 series)[b]	47	66	63	49	18	31	50
2. Short list of leading, coincident, and lagging indicators (25 series)	70	66	67	83	61	76	69
3. Other series, not on full list (34 series)	60	58	67	68	47	62	56
4. All series (120 series)[b]	62	62	66	72	48	62	61

[a] Smoothness and currency weighted one-half each; other criteria weighted one each.
[b] Export orders of durables and export orders of machinery omitted because complete set of measures is not available.

deal with it here again.[6] In addition the more specific question is asked as to what improvements take place when a revised list of National Bureau indicators is released. In each report in which a revised list has been released, an appraisal of the previous list, as well as the new list, has been made. This will also be done here.

A comparison of the old and new list can be made in terms of their aggregate performance and in terms of the individual series.

First, let us consider how well the 1960 list performed in the period after which it was compiled. Table 11 shows the timing of the 1960 list of indicators prior to and subsequent to their selection. The principal finding from this table is that the timing behavior of the series at the two business cycle turning points that have taken place since the list was initially compiled (the May 1960 peak and the February 1961 trough) is essentially the same as in the earlier period. Eleven of the 12 leading series led at the 1960 peak; one failed to reach a peak. Their performance was less uniform in this respect at the 1961 trough: 7 led, 3 coincided, and 2 experienced no turning point. The median lead at the 1960 peak was longer than the median at earlier peaks and the median at the 1961 trough was shorter. With a few exceptions, the roughly coincident series met the standards for that class. Three series, personal income, bank debits outside New York, and wholesale price index (excluding farm products and foods) skipped the mild 1960–61 recession entirely; also, there was a predominance of leads at the peak. Among the lagging indicators, there was a clear predominance of lags at both turns.

Thus the three groups of indicators in the 1960 list exhibited some variation from their expected pattern, but for the most part it was well within the range of earlier variations, as can be seen from the table. Counting up the number of timing observations that are con-

[6] See, for example, *Business Cycle Indicators*, Vol. I, especially Chaps. 3, 4, and 10; Julius Shiskin, *Signals of Recession and Recovery*, Occasional Paper 77, New York, NBER, 1961, pp. 89–115; Sydney S. Alexander, "Rate of Change Approaches to Forecasting—Diffusion Indexes and First Differences," *Economic Journal*, June 1958, pp. 288–301; Arthur L. Broida, "Diffusion Indexes," *American Statistician*, June 1955, pp. 7–16; Alexander Sachs, "The Cyclical Indicator Approach," *The Conference Board Business Record*, April 1957; Leonard H. Lempert, "On the Value of Cyclical Indicators," *The Conference Board Business Record*, June 1957; Arthur M. Okun, "On the Appraisal of Cyclical Turning Point Predictors," *Journal of Business*, April 1960, pp. 101–120; Donald J. Daly and Derek A. White, "Economic Indicators in the 1960's," and Robert C. Turner, "An Appraisal of Various Approaches to Short-Term Forecasting," *Proceedings of the Business and Economic Statistics Section*, American Statistical Association, 1966, pp. 64–83.

TABLE 11

Timing of 1960 List of Twenty-six Indicators Prior to and Subsequent to Their Selection

	First Business Cycle Turn Covered	Timing at Peaks Through 1957: Range from	Range to	Median	Timing at May 1960 Peak	Timing at Troughs Through 1958: Range from	Range to	Median	Timing at February 1961 Trough
				LEAD(−) OR LAG(+), IN MONTHS					
Leading group									
Average workweek, mfg.	1921	−20	+2	−5	−12	−8	+5	−4½	−2
Gross accession rate, mfg.	1919	−35	−3	−10	−14	−27	0	−4	−4
Layoff rate, mfg. (inv.)	1919	−27	−1	−9	−12	−11	−1	−7	0
New orders, durable goods	1920	−35	−3	−6	−13	−11	0	−2½	−1
Housing starts[a]	1918	−31	+8	−11	−17	−12	0	−6	−2
Comm. and indus. building contracts	1919	−32	+2	−9	n.c.	−5	+3	−1½	n.c.
Net change in bus. pop.	1945	−33	−10	−28	−13	−7	0	−4	−1
Bus. failures, liab. (inv.)	1879	−28	+3	−7	−12	−13	+7	−7	n.c.
Corporate profits after taxes, Q	1920	−20	0	−4	−12	−9	+1	−2	0
Common stock price index	1873	−21	+2	−4	−10	−21	+9	−5	−4
Change in business inventories	1921	−26	+9	−5½	−3	−11	+6	+1	0
Indus. raw materials prices	1919	−29	+3	−7½	−6	−8	+9	0	−2
Median of leading group				−7¼	−12			−4	−1½
Roughly coincident group									
Employment in nonagri. establishments	1929	−15	+2	−2½	−1	−1	+1	0	0
Unemployment rate (inv.)	1929	−6	+2	−4	−11	0	+7	+1½	+3
Industrial production	1919	−15	+5	0	−4	−8	+4	0	0
GNP in current $, Q	1921	−2	+3	+½	0	−3	+4	−1	−3
GNP in constant $, Q	1921	−2	+3	0	−3	−7	+4	−3½	0
Bank debits outside N.Y.C.	1919	−3	+6	0	n.c.	−2	+1	−1	n.c.
Personal income	1921	−5	+9	+1	n.c.	−12	0	−2	n.c.
Sales by retail stores[b]	1919	−4	+6	+1	−1	−7	+8	−1	+2
Wholesale price index, excl. farm prod. & foods	1913	−15	+6	+½	n.c.	0	+7	+1	n.c.
Median of roughly coincident group				0	−2			−1	0
Lagging Group									
Plant & equip. expend., Q	1918	−3	+4	+1	0	−1	+6	+2	+3
Labor cost per unit of output, mfg.[c]	1919	+5	+10	+7½	+10	+3	+24	+9	+[d]
Manufacturers' inventories, book value	1926	−10	+9	+2	+4	−6	+13	+3	+4
Consumer instal. debt	1929	+3	+7	+5½	+8	−2	+6	+3½	+3
Bank rates, bus. loans, Q	1919	−20	+13	+5	−5	+2	+39	+5	+49
Median of lagging group				+5	+4			+3½	+4

n.c. = No timing comparison.

[a] Residential building contracts, 1918–38.

[b] Department store sales, 1919–35.

[c] Production worker wage cost per unit of output, 1919–48.

[d] Length of lag uncertain.

sistent with the series' classification, we find that 69 per cent of the 26 possible timing comparisons were consistent at the 1960 peak, and 69 per cent were consistent at the 1961 trough. This corresponds well with a similar test of the 1950 list of 21 indicators during a period subsequent to their selection, namely, 1948–58. Here 67 per cent were found to be "consistent."[7]

The performance of the indicators may be appraised also by considering the behavior of monthly indexes of the various groupings of indicators classified by their typical timing. Activities such as production, employment, and income are heterogeneous in the sense that they cannot be added to any meaningful total. They are homogeneous, however, in the sense that they measure related aspects of business change and undergo similar cyclical fluctuations. Composite indexes constructed from such series provide single measures of the complex of economic activities which experience common fluctuations. For this reason they are helpful in business cycle studies. Such indexes have been prepared separately for leading, coincident, and lagging indicators, and for the 1960 and 1966 lists (Chart 3).

The measures used for this purpose are "amplitude-adjusted" composite indexes. They are constructed by standardizing the month-to-month percentage changes of each series so that all the series are expressed in comparable units. To do this, each series is adjusted so that its average month-to-month change, without regard to direction, is 1. The individual amplitude-adjusted series are weighted and combined in an index. The weights are the scores earned under the plan described in this paper. This index is also adjusted so that its average month-to-month change is 1. The amplitude-adjusted indexes provide a composite measure of the amplitude and pattern of the business cycle, and indexes for different groups of series and different periods can be compared. In addition, they facilitate the interpretation of current changes: if an index shows an increase of 2.0 in the current month, it is rising twice as fast as its average rate of change in the past; if the increase is 0.5, it is rising only half as fast as the historical average.[8]

[7] *Business Cycle Indicators,* Vol. I, p. 53.

The composite indexes in Chart 3 yield two interesting results. First, the indexes based upon the 1966 list are virtually the same as the corresponding indexes based upon the 1960 list. Many of these graphic similarities are quantified in Table 12. This reflects the fact that on an over-all basis the new and the old lists have many common elements. The advantages of the new list are to be found in the new series themselves, in the scores as aids in utilizing both the new and old series, and in the new cross-classification as a contribution toward understanding their economic interrelationships.

The second major finding revealed by this chart is the pronounced differences in the timing properties and the patterns of the leading, coincident, and lagging indexes. Thus, while the leading indexes are scarcely affected by the change in their composition, and neither are the coincident or lagging indexes, nevertheless the leading indexes are quite different from the coincident indexes, and these, in turn, are quite different from the indexes of the lagging series. The principal differences are in the timing properties—the leading indicators usually turn first, the coincident indicators next, and the lagging indicators last. There are other important differences as well: for example, the indexes of the leading indicators show little upward trend since 1948, while the upward trend in the coincident indicators is pronounced. There has also been an upward trend in the indexes of the lagging series, but this seems to have diminished somewhat since 1961.

These two findings point to considerable similarity in behavior within each group of indicators and considerable difference from group to group, and hence attest to the sig-

[8] Shiskin, *Signals of Recession and Recovery,* Appendix A. For a recent innovation, see Shiskin, "Reverse Trend Adjustment of Leading Indicators," *Review of Economics and Statistics,* February 1967.

CHART 3

Composite Indexes Based on the 1960 and 1966 NBER Lists

Leading Indicators

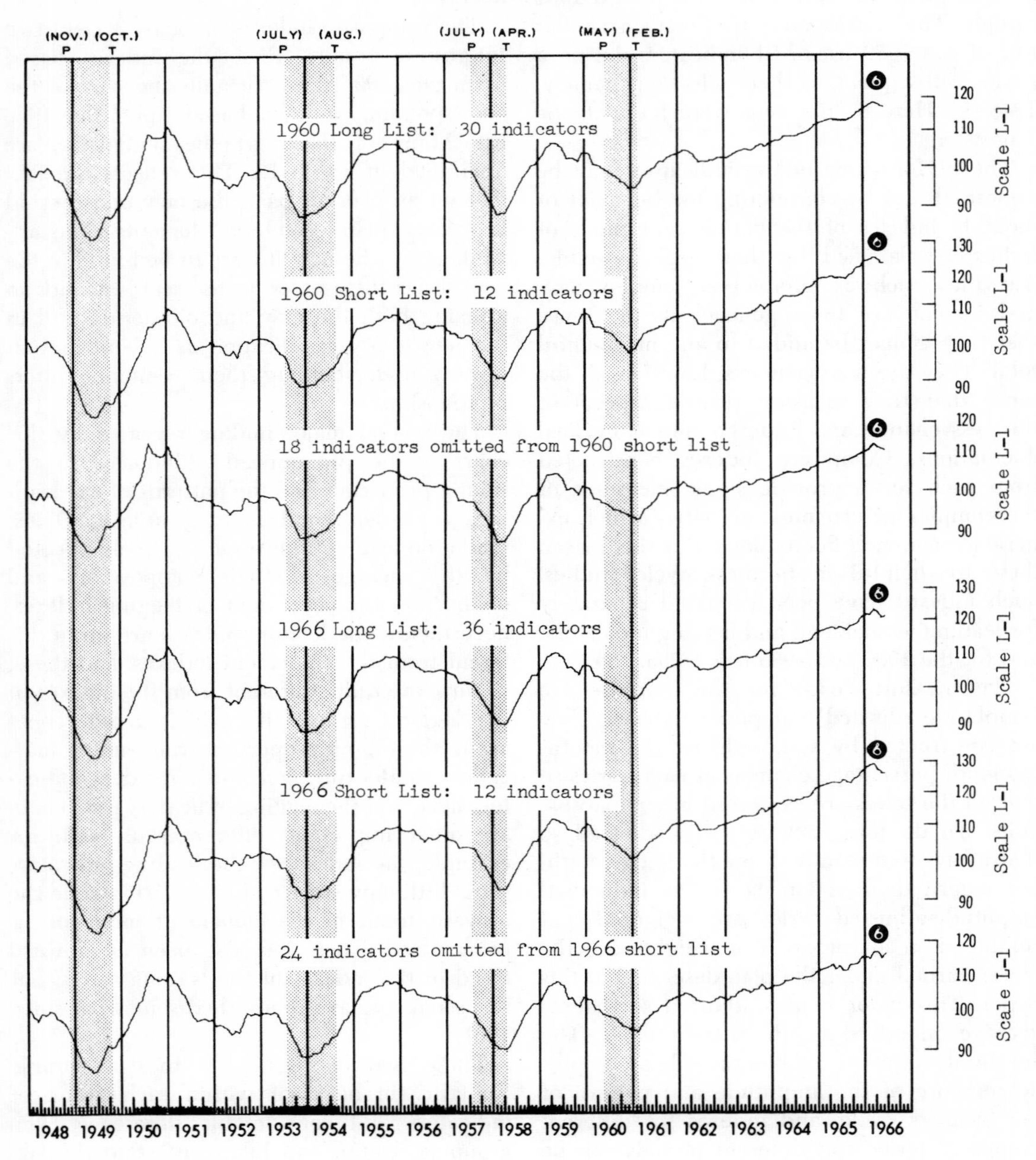

Note: Components are weighted by their average scores. Numbers in dark circles indicate latest month plotted.

CHART 3

Composite Indexes Based on the 1960 and 1966 NBER Lists

Roughly Coincident Indicators

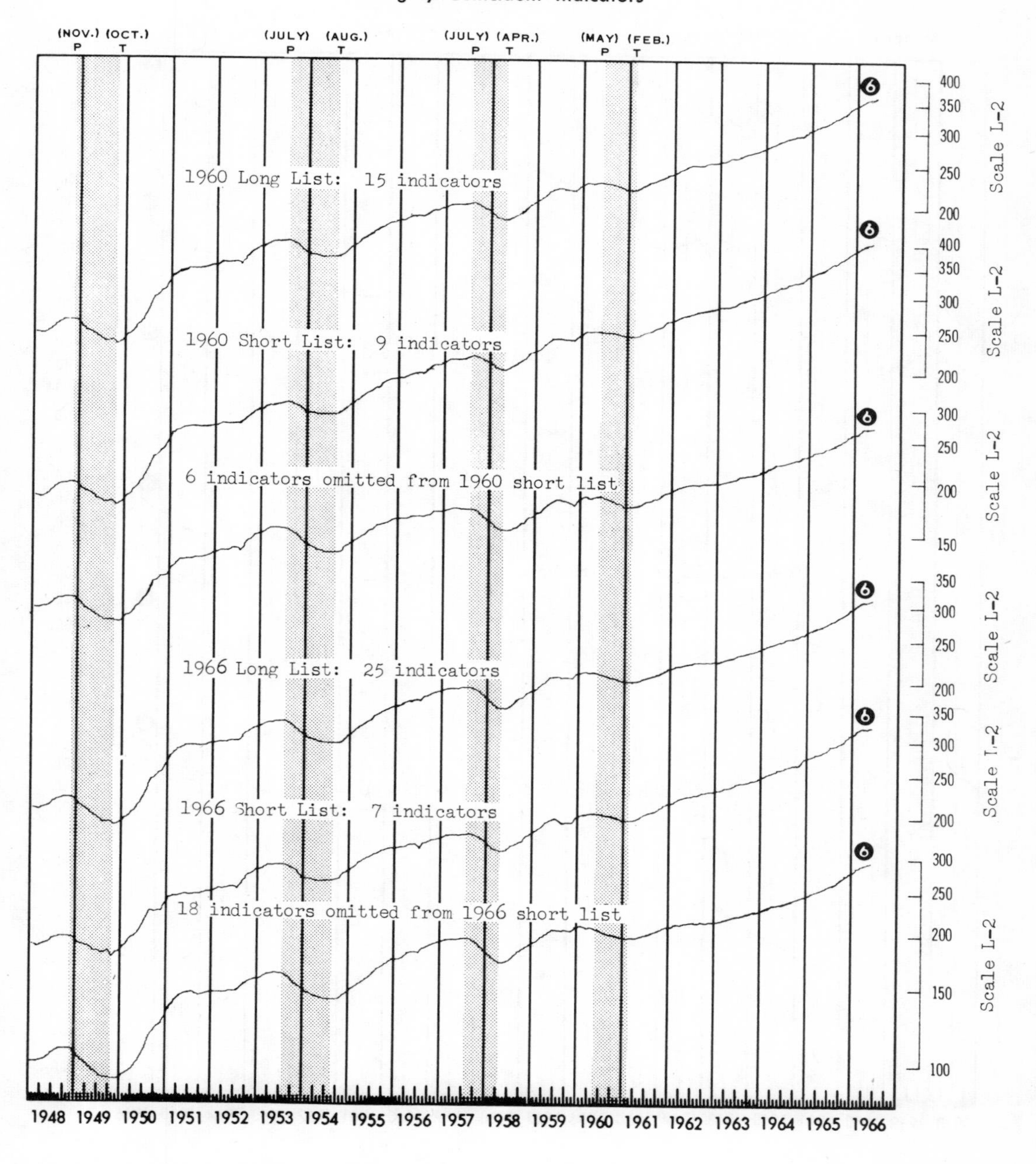

CHART 3

Composite Indexes Based on the 1960 and 1966 NBER Lists

Lagging Indicators

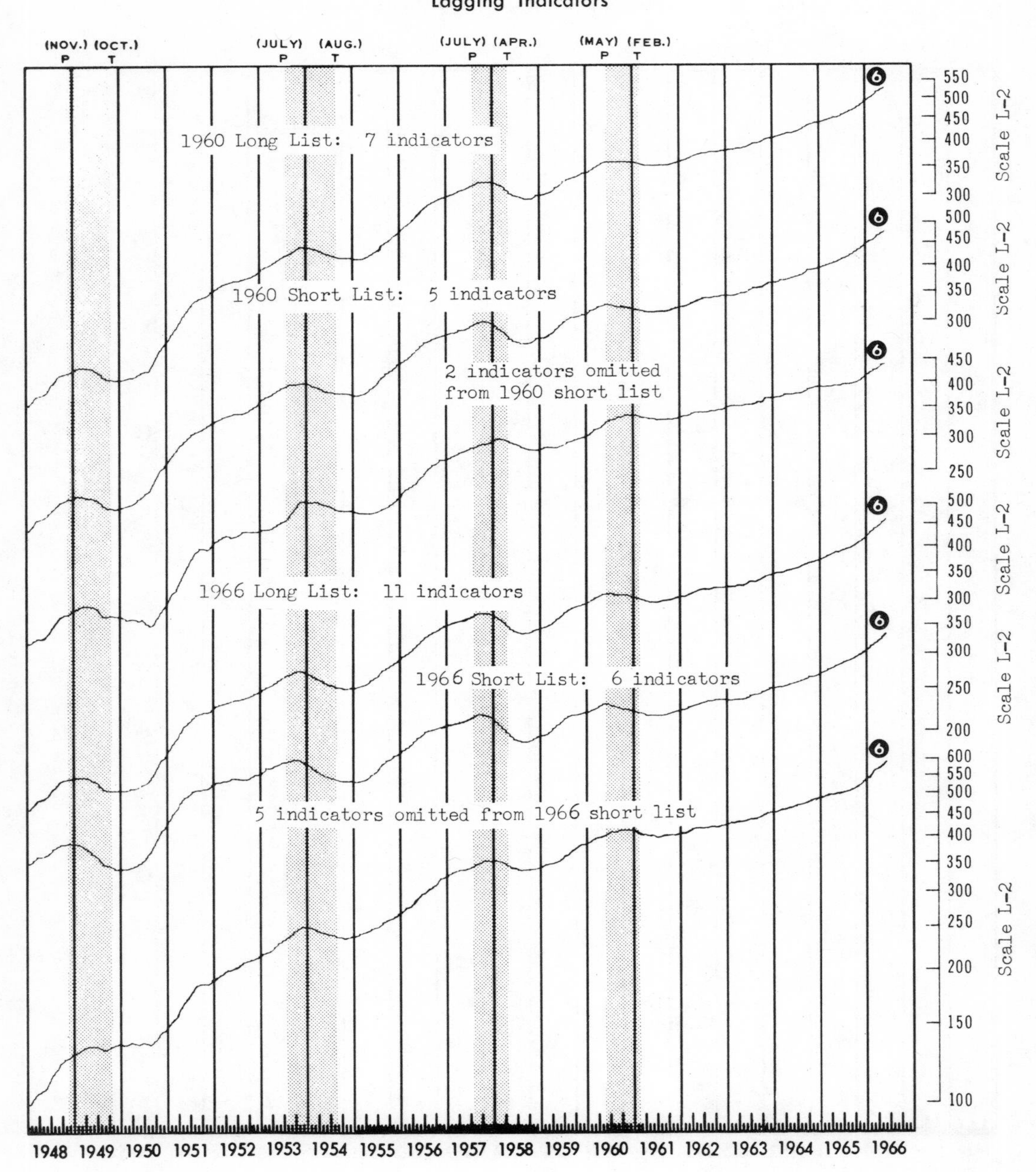

TABLE 12
Summary Measures for Composite Indexes Based on NBER 1960 and 1966 Lists of Indicators, 1948–66

Composite Index	$\overline{CI}$	$\overline{I}$	$\overline{C}$	$\overline{I}/\overline{C}$	MCD	$\overline{I}/\overline{C}$ for MCD Span	Average Duration of Run			
							CI	I	C	MCD
Leading										
1960 long list: 30 indicators	1.00	.52	.76	.69	1	.69	3.4	1.8	12.3	3.4
1960 short list: 12 indicators	.99	.56	.76	.73	1	.73	3.8	1.7	10.1	3.8
18 indicators not on 1960 short list	1.00	.61	.72	.84	1	.84	3.3	1.7	14.8	3.3
1966 long list: 36 indicators	1.00	.56	.76	.73	1	.73	3.0	1.7	12.3	3.0
1966 short list: 12 indicators	.99	.59	.74	.79	1	.79	3.1	1.8	11.1	3.1
24 indicators not on 1966 short list	1.01	.63	.73	.86	1	.86	3.0	1.6	13.9	3.0
Roughly Coincident										
1960 long list: 15 indicators	1.00	.40	.90	.45	1	.45	5.8	1.8	17.1	5.8
1960 short list: 9 indicators	1.01	.42	.90	.47	1	.47	5.3	1.8	17.1	5.3
6 indicators not on 1960 short list	1.00	.48	.86	.56	1	.56	4.4	1.8	20.2	4.4
1966 long list: 25 indicators	1.00	.37	.92	.40	1	.40	5.3	1.8	17.1	5.3
1966 short list: 7 indicators	1.01	.53	.83	.64	1	.64	4.6	1.7	20.2	4.6
18 indicators not on 1966 short list	1.00	.33	.94	.36	1	.36	6.3	1.8	20.2	6.3
Lagging										
1960 long list: 7 indicators	1.01	.29	.97	.30	1	.30	13.9	2.1	24.7	13.9
1960 short list: 5 indicators	1.00	.29	.95	.30	1	.30	11.1	1.9	24.7	11.1
2 indicators not on 1960 short list	1.01	.45	.88	.52	1	.52	4.0	1.9	24.6	4.0
1966 long list: 11 indicators	1.01	.28	.97	.29	1	.29	13.1	1.8	24.7	13.1
1966 short list: 6 indicators	1.01	.33	.95	.35	1	.35	8.9	1.8	20.2	8.9
5 indicators not on 1966 short list	1.01	.39	.93	.42	1	.42	7.7	1.7	20.2	7.7

Note: For a description of these measures, see *Business Cycle Indicators*, Vol. I, pp. 535–545.

nificance of the classification of series into the three timing groups.

Homogeneity in the behavior of different types of series within the leading group is also suggested by a new set of composite indexes that make use of the economic process groupings developed in this study. Chart 4 presents indexes for five of the economic process groups that are classified as leading. Each index is based upon three or four series, selected to provide broad coverage of the particular group without much duplication.[9] The twelve leading indicators on the short list are all included, as well as six additional series, or eighteen in all. These indexes exhibit a rather striking family resemblance in timing as well as in general configuration, despite the variety of economic activities they represent. No one of them is likely to be mistaken for the index of coincident series or for the index of lagging series. One is led, therefore, to conclude that the several economic processes represented in Chart 4 act and react upon one another with greater speed and determination than they do upon the processes represented in the coincident and lagging groups. To the extent that this is plausible, it promotes confidence that the future performance of the new list of indicators will accord well with past performance.

[9] The series included in the five indexes come from the corresponding groups in Table 6, with two exceptions. Series 38 (net business formation) is included in the index of capital investment commitments and series 23 (industrial materials prices) is included in the index of inventory investment and purchasing.

CHART 4

Amplitude-Adjusted Composite Indexes for Economic Subgroups of Leading Indicators

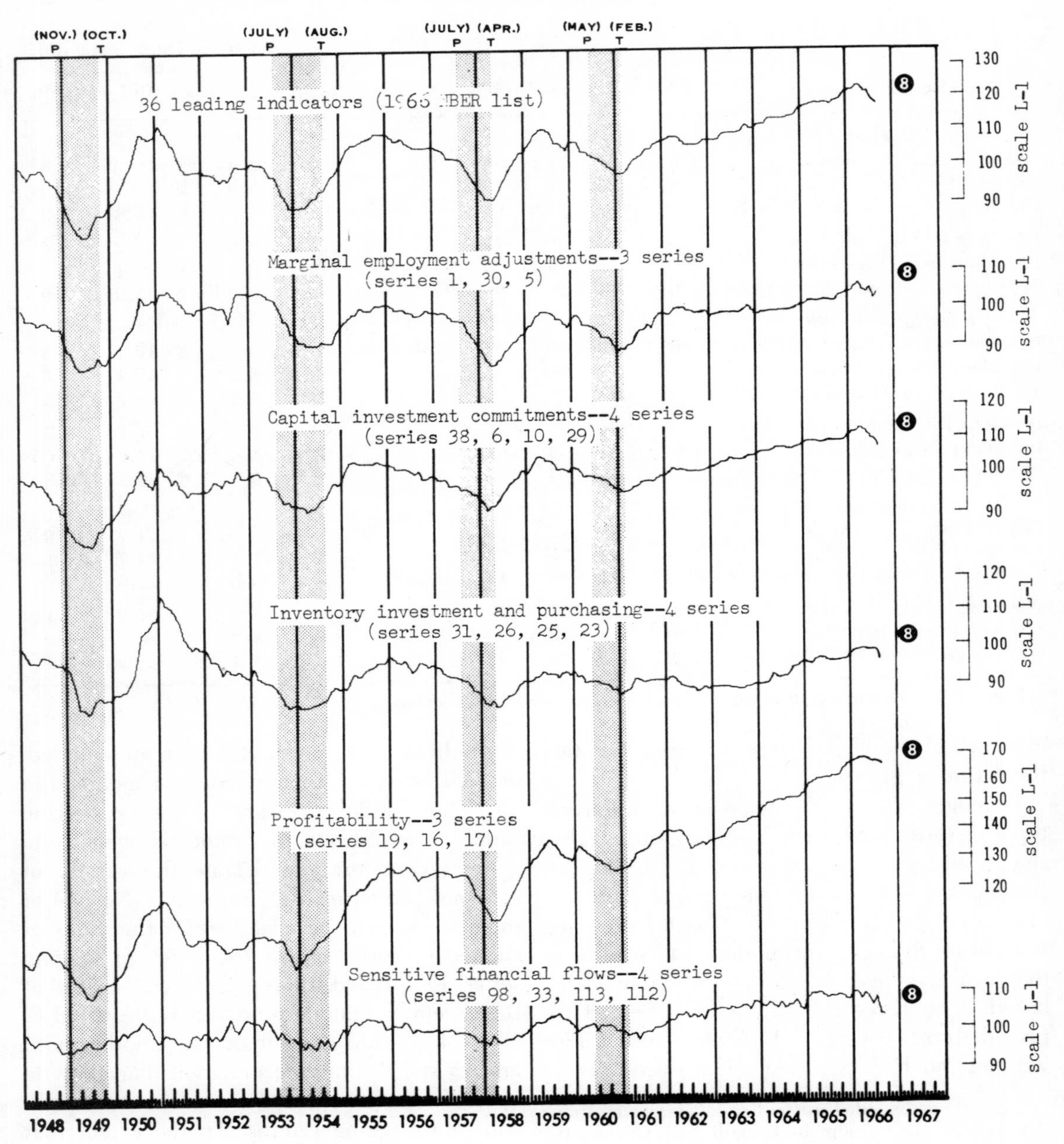

Note: Numbers in dark circles indicate latest month plotted.

APPENDIX A
Instructions for Assigning Scores to Indicators

The rules listed below were used by the staff in making the entries on the scoresheets (cf. text Table 3).

Percentages, in parentheses, following economic significance, statistical adequacy, etc., are the weights assigned to the various measures in computing the final averages (VII).

Timing (IV), conformity (III), and smoothness (VI) scores are based on measures recorded on worksheet tables entitled: *Measures of Timing, Conformity, and Smoothness* (cf. text Table 4). Formulas for timing, dispersion, conformity, and extra turns are computed to one decimal but rounded to whole numbers on the scoresheets (0.5 is rounded to the nearest even number).

The scores cover the full period for which each series is available through 1965. For series that start before 1948, a second scoresheet was prepared, so that the scores for all series can be compared for a common recent period, 1948–65.

I. Economic Significance (20 Per Cent)

Broad coverage (economy wide; nonagricultural; manufacturing and trade; total corporate; commodity, consumption, or investment aggregates).	75
Narrow coverage (manufacturing and other industry groups or sectors at about this or narrower levels of aggregation).	50

See text (Chapter II, 3) for explanation.

II. Statistical Adequacy (20 Per Cent)

	Score	Maximum Score
1. Reporting system		20
a. For statistical purposes	20	
b. Byproduct of administrative program	10	
c. Indirect sources	0	
2. Coverage of process (statistical)		20
a. Full universe (90–100 per cent)	20	
b. Probability sample	15	
c. Other sample (50–90 per cent)	10	
d. Other sample (less than 50 per cent or unspecified)	5	
3. Coverage of time period (full month or quarter)		10
4. Measure of magnitude of revisions		5
5. Measure of error		10
a. Total	10	
b. Sampling	5	
6. Full description of method		5
7. Duration of series		20
a. 50 years or more	20	
b. Each 5 years	2	

	Score	Maximum Score
8. Comparability over time		10
a. No break	6	
b. One break	3	
c. Two breaks	0	
d. Uninterrupted current segment of at least 15 years	4	
9. Total score		100

III. Conformity (20 Per Cent)

	Maximum Score
1. Conformity probability	60

$$\text{Score} = 300\ (.200 - P_C)$$

where P_C is the probability assigned to the weighted conformity indexes for expansions and contractions combined.

2. Extra turns	20

$$\text{Score} = 80\left(0.25 - \frac{E}{T}\right)$$

where E is the number of extra specific cycle turns and T the total number of business cycle turns covered by the whole series. If $\frac{E}{T}$ is greater than 0.25, the score is zero.

3. Lapses since 1948	10

Series analyzed on a positive (inverted) basis are considered to have no lapses if they always rise (decline) during business cycle expansions and decline (rise) during business cycle contractions. No change in a series during a business cycle phase is counted as one-half expanding and one-half contracting.

Series covering the period 1948–65 should have 3 expansions and 4 contractions. Shorter series may show fewer expansions and contractions. They are scored by applying a modification of the formula used for "conformity probability"

$$\text{Score} = 52\ (.200 - P_{CL})$$

where P_{CL} is the probability for the number of conforming movements.

4. Amplitude	10

Amplitude is based on the weighted average per month rise and fall during specific cycles.[1]

[1] The average per month rise and fall of all specific cycles available for a series is used in scoring amplitude. The per month rather than the total amplitudes are used because series cover different periods. Thus a series which covers the 1929–33 contraction is almost certain to have a larger average cyclical amplitude than one which does not, but it is not certain to have a larger per month amplitude. This measure is considered preferable to $\overline{C}$ (the Census seasonal

Maximum Score

Scoring is as follows for series analyzed on a relative basis:

Amplitude	*Score*
4.0 or more	10
3.0 to 3.99	8
2.0 to 2.99	6
1.0 to 1.99	4
0.5 to 0.99	2
Less than 0.5	0

Series analyzed on an absolute deviation basis automatically score 8.

5. Total score — 100

IV. Timing (20 Per Cent)

1. At business cycle peaks
   a. Probability — 60

$$\text{Score} = 240\ (0.250 - P)$$

where P represents the accepted probability based on peak timing. If P is larger than 0.250, the score will be zero.

Any timing class (lead, lag, roughly coincident) that yields an accepted probability is to be identified. However, when the median lead or lag is -1, 0, or $+1$ month, the timing class is C provided the probability attaching to the number of rough coincidences is "accepted." Otherwise, it is U. When the median lead (or lag) is -2 (or $+2$) months or more, the timing class is L (or Lg) provided the probability attaching to the number of leads (or lags) is "accepted." If the probability is rejected for leads (or lags) but accepted for rough coincidences, then the timing class is C. Otherwise, it is U. Scores for probability and lapses, for the timing classification rejected under the foregoing rules, are to be recorded in a footnote.

   b. Dispersion — 20

Score = 2 (10 — σ of the leads and lags at peaks)
If σ is 10 or more the score is 0

   c. Lapses since 1948 — 20

Series covering the full period 1948–65 should have 4 comparisons at peaks and 4 comparisons at troughs. Shorter series may show fewer comparisons.

adjustment Method II measure of the average month-to-month change, without regard to sign, in a smooth moving average of the cyclical component of the series) because the NBER measure excludes minor cycles and the long-term trend; furthermore, the NBER measure is more often available for the full period covered by the series. For 93 series for which both are available, the coefficient of rank correlation between these two measures of amplitude is 0.823.

Scoring is computed by applying a modification of the probability formula to the classification scored for "probability."

$$\text{Score} = 93\ (.250 - P_{CL})$$

d. Total score — $\overline{100}$

2. At business cycle troughs
   Computations correspond to those for peaks. — 100
3. At peaks and troughs
   Score is an arithmetic average of the scores for peaks and for troughs. Thus, the score is not necessarily representative of the classification shown for peaks and troughs combined in Table 6. — 100

V. Currency (10 Per Cent)

	Score	*Maximum Score*
Monthly Series		100
Promptness: Available by 20th of month following that covered by data	80	
Available by 20th of 2nd month following that covered by data	40	
Available later	0	
Daily, weekly, or ten-day figures in addition to monthly figure	20	
Quarterly Series		50
Available in month following quarter	50	
Available in second month following quarter	25	
Available later	0	

VI. Smoothness (10 Per Cent)

Monthly Series — 100

MCD	*Score*
1	100
2	80
3	60
4	40
5	20
6 or more	0

Quarterly Series — 100

$\bar{I}/\bar{C}$	*Score*
Less than .33	100
.33 – .66	80
.67 – .99	60
1.00 – 1.33	40
1.34 – 1.66	20
1.67 or more	0

VII. Summary—Average Score (100 Per Cent)

1. Peaks (troughs)

   Average to be computed by weighting the score for peak (trough) timing (IV) and the scores for the remaining measures (I, II, etc.) by the percentages indicated in the headings.

2. Peaks and troughs

   Same computation as above except that peak and trough timing score (IV-3) is to be used.

   The timing classification on which the score is based is to be identified together with the score.

Appendix B
Eighty-eight Selected Indicators Classified by Timing and Economic Process: Timing Characteristics for Peaks and Troughs Separately

Classification and Series Title (1)	At Peaks (P) or Troughs (T) (2)	Number of: Business Cycle Turns Covered (3)	Leads (4)	Rough Coincidences[a] (5)	Lags (6)	Timing Comparisons (7)	Business Cycle Turns Skipped (8)	Extra Specific Cycle Turns (9)	Median Lead(−) or Lag(+) in Months (10)	Timing Class[b] (11)	% in Timing Class (12)
LEADING INDICATORS (36 SERIES)											
1. Employment and unemployment											
Marginal employment adjustments											
*1. Avg. workweek, prod. workers, mfg.	P	9	7	1(0)	1	8	1	1	−6	L	78
	T	10	6	3(2)	1	9	1	1	−4	L	60
*30. Nonagri. placements, BES	P	5	4	0(0)	0	4	1	2	−11	L	80
	T	5	4	4(0)	1	5	0	2	−1	C	80
2. Accession rate, mfg.	P	10	10	2(0)	0	10	0	3	−10	L	100
	T	11	9	4(2)	0	11	0	3	−4	L	82
5. Initial claims, unempl. insur. (inv.)	P	5	4	0(0)	0	4	1	1	−18	L	80
	T	5	2	4(2)	1	5	0	1	0	C	80
3. Layoff rate, mfg. (inv.)	P	10	10	2(0)	0	10	0	2	−10	L	100
	T	11	9	4(1)	0	10	1	2	−6	L	82
3. Fixed capital investment											
Formation of business enterprises											
*38. Index of net business formation	P	5	4	0(0)	0	4	1	0	−20	L	80
	T	5	4	3(1)	0	5	0	0	−3	L	80
13. New business incorporations	P	25	15	8(1)	4	20	5	8	−4	L	60
	T	25	18	5(1)	3	22	3	7	−6	L	72
New investment commitments											
*6. New orders, dur. goods indus.	P	10	8	1(0)	0	8	2	1	−8	L	80
	T	10	8	6(1)	0	9	1	1	−2	L	80
94. Construction contracts, total, value	P	13	9	3(0)	1	10	3	5	−8	L	69
	T	13	10	5(1)	0	11	2	5	−4	L	77
*10. Contracts and orders, plant and equip.	P	4	4	0(0)	0	4	0	0	−8	L	100
	T	4	3	2(0)	1	4	0	0	−3	L	75
11. New capital appropriations, mfg., Q	P	3	2	1(0)	1	3	0	0	−6	U	

Series											
	T	4	4	2(0)	0	4	0	0	−4	L	100
9. Constr. contracts, comm. and indus., floor area	P	10	6	2(0)	1	7	3	2	−9	L	60
	T	11	5	6(1)	2	8	3	2	−2	U	
7. Private nonfarm housing starts	P	11	8	1(0)	1	9	2	3	−13	L	73
	T	11	9	4(1)	0	10	1	3	−5	L	82
*29. New building permits, private housing units	P	11	8	1(0)	1	9	2	4	−13	L	73
	T	11	9	4(1)	0	10	1	4	−5	L	82
4. Inventories and inventory investment											
Inventory investment and purchasing											
21. Change in business inventories, all indus., Q	P	9	6	4(0)	3	9	0	2	−3	L	67
	T	10	4	4(1)	5	10	0	2	0	U	
*31. Change in book value, mfg. and trade inventories	P	5	5	0(0)	0	5	0	2	−14	L	100
	T	5	4	2(1)	0	5	0	2	−6	L	80
37. Purchased materials, % reptg. higher inventories	P	4	4	0(0)	0	4	0	2	−8	L	100
	T	4	2	3(1)	1	4	0	2	−2	C	75
20. Change in bk. val., mfrs.' inventories of mat. and supp.	P	5	4	1(0)	0	4	1	2	−16	L	80
	T	5	4	3(0)	1	5	0	1	−3	L	80
26. Buying policy, mater., % reptg. commitments 60+ days	P	3	3	0(0)	0	3	0	2	−12	L	100
	T	3	3	3(0)	0	3	0	2	−2	L	100
32. Vendor performance, % reptg. slower deliveries	P	4	4	1(0)	0	4	0	1	−10	L	100
	T	4	4	0(0)	0	4	0	2	−8	L	100
25. Change in unfilled orders, dur. goods indus.	P	5	5	0(0)	0	5	0	1	−19	L	100
	T	5	5	2(0)	0	5	0	1	−6	L	100
5. Prices, costs, and profits											
Sensitive commodity price indexes											
*23. Industrial materials prices	P	10	8	3(0)	1	9	1	2	−6	L	80
	T	11	5	6(4)	1	10	1	2	0	U	
Stock price indexes											
*19. Stock prices, 500 common stocks	P	22	17	9(1)	2	20	2	4	−4	L	77
	T	22	16	5(1)	3	20	2	4	−4	L	73
Profits and profit margins											
*16. Corporate profits after taxes, Q	P	10	7	4(2)	0	9	1	2	−6	L	70
	T	10	6	7(2)	2	10	0	2	−2	L	60
22. Ratio, profits to income orig., corp., all indus., Q	P	4	4	0(0)	0	4	0	1	−16	L	100
	T	4	3	2(1)	0	4	0	1	−4	L	75
18. Profits per dollar of sales, corporate, mfg., Q	P	4	4	1(0)	0	4	0	1	−16	L	100
	T	4	3	2(1)	0	4	0	1	−4	L	75
*17. Ratio, price to unit labor cost, mfg.	P	10	9	4(0)	1	10	0	1	−11	L	90
	T	11	8	6(1)	2	11	0	1	−3	L	73

Appendix B (*Continued*)

Classification and Series Title (1)	At Peaks (P) or Troughs (T) (2)	Number of: Business Cycle Turns Covered (3)	Leads (4)	Rough Coincidences[a] (5)	Lags (6)	Timing Comparisons (7)	Business Cycle Turns Skipped (8)	Extra Specific Cycle Turns (9)	Median Lead(−) or Lag(+) in Months (10)	Timing Class[b] (11)	% in Timing Class (12)
LEADING INDICATORS (CONCLUDED)											
6. Money and credit											
Flows of money and credit											
98. Change in money supply and time	P	13	12	0(0)	0	12	1	2	−20	L	92
deposits[c]	T	14	12	0(0)	1	13	1	2	−11	L	86
85. Change in money supply[c]	P	11	10	0(0)	0	10	1	1	−20	L	91
	T	12	9	1(0)	1	10	2	1	−10	L	75
110. Total private borrowing, Q	P	3	3	0(0)	0	3	0	0	−12	L	100
	T	3	1	2(1)	1	3	0	0	0	U	
*113. Change in consumer instalment debt	P	7	6	1(0)	0	6	1	2	−12	L	86
	T	7	5	3(0)	1	6	1	2	−4	L	71
112. Change in bank loans to businesses	P	5	4	0(0)	0	4	1	1	−22	L	80
	T	6	2	4(2)	1	5	1	1	0	C	67
33. Change in mortgage debt	P	2	2	0(0)	0	2	0	0	−18[j]	L	100
	T	2	1	1(1)	0	2	0	0	−4[j]	U	
Credit difficulties											
14. Liabilities of bus. failures (inv.)	P	21	15	3(1)	2	18	3	1	−10	L	71
	T	22	16	2(1)	1	18	4	1	−7	L	73
39. Delinquency rate, instal. loans, 30+ days	P	4	4	2(0)	0	4	0	0	−6	L	100
(inv.)	T	4	2	3(0)	2	4	0	0	0	C	75
ROUGHLY COINCIDENT INDICATORS (25 SERIES)											
1. Employment and unemployment											
Job vacancies											
301. Nonagri. job openings, number pending,	P	4	3	0(0)	0	3	1	1	−8	L	75
BES	T	4	0	4(2)	2	4	0	1	0	C	100
46. Help-wanted advertising	P	10	5	4(2)	2	9	1	0	−3	L	50

Series											
Comprehensive employment series											
501. Man-hours in nonfarm establishments,	P	5	5	3(0)	0	5	0	0	−1	U	
employees	T	5	1	5(2)	2	5	0	0	0	C	100
*41. Employees in nonagri. establishments[d]	P	7	5	5(1)	1	7	0	0	−2	L	71
	T	7	1	7(5)	1	7	0	0	0	C	100
42. Total nonagri. employment	P	5	3	2(0)	2	5	0	0	−4	U	
	T	5	4	5(1)	0	5	0	0	−1	C	100
Comprehensive unemployment series											
*43. Unemployment rate, total (inv.)	P	7	4	2(1)	1	6	1	0	−4	L	57
	T	7	0	6(2)	5	7	0	0	+2	Lg	71
45. Insured unemployment rate (inv.)	P	3	3	1(0)	0	3	0	2	−11	L	100
	T	4	0	4(2)	2	4	0	2	0	C	100
40. Unemployment rate, married males (inv.)	P	2	2	0(0)	0	2	0	0	−15[j]	L	100
	T	2	0	2(0)	2	2	0	0	+2[j]	Lg	100
2. Production, income, consumption, and trade											
Comprehensive production series											
49. GNP in current dollars, expenditure	P	9	1	7(3)	3	7	2	0	0	C	78
estimate, Q	T	10	5	7(0)	3	8	2	0	−1	C	70
*50. GNP in constant dollars, expenditure	P	8	2	6(2)	2	6	2	0	0	C	75
estimate, Q	T	9	5	3(1)	1	7	2	0	−3	L	56
*47. Industrial production[e]	P	10	5	5(3)	2	10	0	0	0	U	
	T	11	4	8(6)	1	11	0	0	0	C	73
Comprehensive income series											
*52. Personal income	P	9	2	5(1)	5	8	1	0	+1	U	
	T	10	8	7(1)	0	9	1	0	−2	L	80
53. Labor income in mining, mfg., and constr.	P	7	3	6(3)	1	7	0	0	0	C	86
	T	7	1	6(3)	3	7	0	0	0	C	86
Comprehensive consumption and trade series											
57. Final sales in current dollars, Q	P	9	1	2(0)	6	7	2	0	+4	Lg	67
	T	10	5	5(0)	3	8	2	0	−2	U	
*816. Mfg. and trade sales	P	4	3	2(1)	0	4	0	1	−4	L	75
	T	4	1	4(3)	0	4	0	1	0	C	100
*54. Sales of retail stores	P	10	2	3(0)	4	6	4	0	+1	U	
	T	11	3	4(1)	2	6	5	0	0	U	
3. Fixed capital investment											
Backlog of investment commitments											
96. Mfrs.' unfilled orders, dur. goods indus.	P	5	5	0(0)	0	5	0	1	−7	L	100
	T	5	1	4(1)	3	5	0	1	+1	C	80
97. Backlog of cap. appropriations, mfg., Q	P	3	2	1(0)	0	2	1	0	−6[j]	U	
	T	3	0	1(0)	3	3	0	0	+7	Lg	100

Appendix B (*Continued*)

Classification and Series Title (1)	At Peaks (P) or Troughs (T) (2)	Business Cycle Turns Covered (3)	Number of: Leads (4)	Number of: Rough Coincidences[a] (5)	Number of: Lags (6)	Number of: Timing Comparisons (7)	Number of: Business Cycle Turns Skipped (8)	Number of: Extra Specific Cycle Turns (9)	Median Lead(−) or Lag(+) in Months (10)	Timing Class[b] (11)	% in Timing Class (12)
ROUGHLY COINCIDENT INDICATORS (CONCLUDED)											
5. Prices, costs, and profits											
Comprehensive wholesale price indexes											
55. Wholesale prices exc. farm products and foods	P	12	2	4(1)	3	6	6	1	0	U	
	T	12	0	6(1)	6	7	5	1	+1	U	
58. Wholesale price index, mfd. goods	P	12	4	2(0)	3	7	5	1	−1	U	
	T	12	3	5(1)	4	8	4	1	0	U	
6. Money and credit											
Money market interest rates											
114. Treasury bill rate	P	10	7	5(0)	1	8	2	1	−2	L	70
	T	10	3	5(0)	5	8	2	1	+2	U	
116. Corporate bond yields	P	4	3	3(0)	1	4	0	0	−2	L	75
	T	4	1	1(0)	3	4	0	0	+4	Lg	75
115. Treasury bond yields	P	10	6	4(1)	2	9	1	2	−1	U	
	T	11	1	5(2)	6	9	2	2	+3	Lg	55
117. Municipal bond yields[f]	P	10	5	3(0)	5	10	0	2	0	U	
	T	11	2	5(1)	8	11	0	2	+4	Lg	73
Bank reserves											
93. Free reserves (inv.)[g]	P	7	4	3(0)	1	5	2	1	−1	U	
	T	7	1	3(1)	2	4	3	2	+2	U	
LAGGING INDICATORS (11 SERIES)											
1. Employment and unemployment											
Long-duration unemployment											
*502. Unempl. rate, persons unempl. 15+ weeks (inv.)	P	4	1	3(1)	2	4	0	0	+1	C	75
	T	4	0	2(0)	4	4	0	0	+2	Lg	100
3. Fixed capital investment											
Investment expenditures											
*61. Bus. expend., new plant and equip., Q	P	10	1	9(4)	5	10	0	0	0	C	90
	T	10	1	7(1)	8	10	0	0	+2	Lg	80

Series											
expend.	T	4	0	4(0)	4	4	0	0	+2	Lg	100
4. Inventories and inventory investment											
Inventories											
*71. Book value, mfg. and trade inventories	P	5	1	3(0)	4	5	0	1	+2	Lg	80
	T	5	1	4(0)	4	5	0	1	+2	Lg	80
65. Book value of mfrs.' inventories, finished goods	P	5	1	1(0)	4	5	0	1	+5	Lg	80
	T	6	1	2(0)	5	6	0	1	+4	Lg	83
5. Prices, costs, and profits											
Unit labor costs											
68. Labor cost per dollar of real corp. GNP, Q[h]	P	4	1	1(0)	3	4	0	0	+6	Lg	75
	T	4	0	0(0)	4	4	0	0	+7	Lg	100
*62. Labor cost per unit of output, mfg.[h]	P	10	0	0(0)	7	7	3	1	+8	Lg	70
	T	11	0	1(0)	7	7	4	1	+9	Lg	64
6. Money and credit											
Outstanding debt											
66. Consumer instalment debt	P	7	0	1(0)	5	5	2	2	+6	Lg	71
	T	7	1	3(0)	4	5	2	2	+3	U	
*72. Comm. and indus. loans outstanding	P	6	1	3(0)	3	4	2	1	+2	U	
	T	6	0	3(0)	4	4	2	1	+2	Lg	67
Interest rates on business loans and mortgages											
*67. Bank rates on short-term bus. loans, Q[h]	P	10	2	2(1)	6	9	1	1	+5	Lg	60
	T	11	0	3(0)	9	9	2	1	+5	Lg	82
118. Mortgage yields, residential[h]	P	4	1	3(0)	3	4	0	0	+2	Lg	75
	T	4	0	0(0)	3	3	1	0	+6	Lg	75
OTHER SELECTED SERIES (16 SERIES)											
5. Prices, costs, and profits											
Comprehensive retail price indexes											
81. Consumer price index	P	12	2	2(1)	4	7	5	0	+4	U	
	T	12	0	3(0)	7	7	5	0	+10	Lg	58
7. Foreign trade and payments											
89. U.S. balance of payments, Q	P	5	2	0(0)	0	2	3	6	−6[j]	U	
	T	5	1	1(0)	1	2	3	6	+6[j]	U	
88. Merchandise trade balance (inv.)	P	23	8	11(4)	6	18	5	16	0	U	
	T	24	6	5(0)	7	13	11	21	+1	U	
86. Exports, exc. military aid	P	23	5	2(0)	4	9	14	14	−4	U	
	T	24	4	4(2)	5	11	13	13	0	U	
861. Export orders, durable goods[i]	P	No timing comparisons								U	
	T									U	
862. Export orders, machinery	P	2	0	0(0)	0	0	2	0	—	U	
	T	2	0	0(0)	1	1	1	0	+4[j]	U	

Appendix B (*Concluded*)

Classification and Series Title (1)	At Peaks (P) or Troughs (T) (2)	Business Cycle Turns Covered (3)	Number of: Leads (4)	Number of: Rough Coincidences[a] (5)	Number of: Lags (6)	Number of: Timing Comparisons (7)	Number of: Business Cycle Turns Skipped (8)	Number of: Extra Specific Cycle Turns (9)	Median Lead(−) or Lag(+) in Months (10)	Timing Class[b] (11)	% in Timing Class (12)
OTHER SELECTED SERIES (CONCLUDED)											
87. General imports	P	23	6	11(2)	10	18	5	5	+1	U	
	T	24	11	12(2)	6	19	5	5	−2	U	
8. Federal government activities											
95. Fed. surplus or deficit, inc. and prod. acct., Q	P	4	4	1(0)	0	4	0	1	−14	L	100
	T	4	1	1(0)	3	4	0	1	+2	Lg	75
84. Fed. cash surplus or deficit	P	21	8	5(2)	7	17	4	3	0	U	
	T	22	7	8(1)	10	18	4	3	+2	U	
83. Fed. cash receipts from public	P	21	8	9(5)	5	18	3	0	0	U	
	T	22	7	8(2)	9	18	4	0	0	U	
82. Fed. cash payments to public	P	21	4	5(2)	5	11	10	6	0	U	
	T	22	6	2(0)	4	10	12	7	−4	U	
101. Natl. defense purch., GNP component, current dollars, Q	P	4	1	1(0)	1	2	2	2	+4[j]	U	
	T	4	0	0(0)	2	2	2	3	+10[j]	U	
91. Defense Dept. oblig., total	P	3	2	0(0)	0	2	1	2	−17[j]	U	
	T	3	3	0(0)	0	3	0	2	−10	L	100
90. Defense Dept. oblig., procurement	P	3	2	0(0)	0	2	1	2	−18[j]	U	
	T	3	3	0(0)	0	3	0	2	−9	L	100
99. New orders, defense products	P	3	1	0(0)	0	1	2	0	−11[j]	U	
	T	3	2	0(0)	0	2	1	0	−10[j]	U	
92. Military contract awards in U.S.	P	3	2	0(0)	0	2	1	1	−14[j]	U	
	T	[illegible]	[illegible]	[illegible]	[illegible]	[illegible]	[illegible]	[illegible]	[illegible]	[illegible]	[illegible]

* On short list of indicators (25 series).

[a] Rough coincidences include exact coincidences (shown in parentheses) and leads and lags of 3 months or less. Leads (lags) include leads (lags) of 1 month or more. The total number of timing comparisons, which can be less than the number of business cycle turns covered by the series, is the sum of the leads, exact coincidences, and lags. Leads and lags of quarterly series are expressed in terms of months.

[b] The classification for individual series is based on the median lead or lag plus a probability test applied to the number of leads, rough coincidences, or lags relative to the number of business cycle turns covered.

[c] Also analyzed invertedly, in which case the series is classed as lagging.

[d] Earlier segment omitted, 1914–28 (production worker employment).

[e] Earlier segment omitted, 1890–1918 (volume of business activity, Babson).

[f] Earlier segment omitted, 1857–1918.

[g] Also analyzed positively, in which case the series is classed as lagging.

[h] Also analyzed invertedly, in which case the series is classed as leading.

[i] Data not available before October 1962.

[j] Based on fewer than 3 timing comparisons.

Appendix C
Thirty-four Other Series Classified by Economic Process: Timing Characteristics for Peaks and Troughs Separately

Economic Process and Series Title (1)	At Peaks (P) or Troughs (T) (2)	Number of: Business Cycle Turns Covered (3)	Leads (4)	Rough Coincidences[a] (5)	Lags (6)	Timing Comparisons (7)	Business Cycle Turns Skipped (8)	Extra Specific Cycle Turns (9)	Median Lead(−) or Lag(+) in Months (10)	Timing Class[b] (11)	% in Timing Class (12)
1. Employment and unemployment											
Marginal employment adjustments											
805. Accession rate, new hires, mfg.	P	3	3	0(0)	0	3	0	1	−14	L	100
	T	3	2	2(1)	0	3	0	2	−1	U	
806. Accession rate, rehires, mfg. (inv.)[c]	P	3	3	1(0)	0	3	0	0	−6	L	100
	T	3	0	2(0)	3	3	0	1	+3	Lg	100
4. No. of persons on temporary layoff (inv.)	P	4	3	0(0)	0	3	1	0	−13	L	75
	T	4	2	3(2)	0	4	0	0	0	C	75
Job vacancies											
809. Help-wanted display ads, exec. positions	P	2	2	0(0)	0	2	0	1	−10[e]	L	100
	T	3	3	1(0)	0	3	0	1	−4	L	100
Employment											
801. Man-hours, nonagri. employees, persons with a job	P	5	4	0(0)	0	4	1	0	−4	L	80
	T	5	2	4(1)	1	4	1	0	0	C	80
802. Man-hours, nonagri. employees, persons at work	P	5	4	0(0)	0	4	1	0	−4	L	80
	T	5	2	4(1)	1	4	1	0	0	C	80
807. Nonagri. empl., commodity-producing indus.	P	5	5	2(0)	0	5	0	0	−7	L	100
	T	5	0	4(3)	2	5	0	0	0	C	80
808. Nonagri. empl., service indus.	P	5	0	3(0)	3	3	2	0	+1	U	
	T	5	1	2(1)	1	3	2	0	0	U	
Unemployment											
803. Unemployment rate, under 5 weeks (inv.)	P	4	3	2(1)	0	4	0	2	−2	L	75
	T	4	3	3(1)	0	4	0	2	−2	L	75

810. GNP in current dollars, income estimate, Q	P	5	1	5(2)	2	5	0	0	0	C	100
	T	5	2	4(1)	2	5	0	0	0	C	80
811. GNP in constant dollars, income estimate, Q	P	4	1	4(2)	1	4	0	0	0	C	100
	T	4	1	4(1)	2	4	0	0	0	C	100
814. Steel ingot production	P	16	9	7(2)	5	16	0	0	−1	U	
	T	16	9	10(5)	2	16	0	0	−1	C	62
813. Auto production, passenger cars	P	11	4	4(2)	3	9	2	3	0	U	
	T	11	4	5(1)	4	9	2	2	0	U	
Consumption and trade											
51. Bank debits outside N.Y.C.[d]	P	10	2	5(2)	2	6	4	0	0	U	
	T	11	4	6(1)	1	6	5	0	−1	U	
812. Final sales in constant dollars, Q	P	4	0	1(0)	2	2	2	0	+2[e]	U	
	T	4	2	2(0)	0	2	2	0	−2[e]	U	
503. Manufacturers' sales, total	P	8	3	5(3)	1	7	1	0	0	C	62
	T	8	3	6(2)	2	7	1	0	0	C	75
56. Wholesale sales, merchant wholesalers	P	9	6	6(2)	0	8	1	1	−2	L	67
	T	9	5	4(1)	2	8	1	1	−2	L	56
815. Index of truck tonnage hauled	P	4	3	2(1)	0	4	0	1	−4	L	75
	T	4	4	2(0)	0	4	0	1	−4	L	100
817. Personal consumption expend., dur. goods, Q	P	5	3	3(1)	0	4	1	3	−2	L	60
	T	5	2	2(1)	1	4	1	3	−3	U	

Appendix C (*Concluded*)

Economic Process and Series Title (1)	At Peaks (P) or Troughs (T) (2)	Number of: Business Cycle Turns Covered (3)	Leads (4)	Rough Coincidences[a] (5)	Lags (6)	Timing Comparisons (7)	Business Cycle Turns Skipped (8)	Extra Specific Cycle Turns (9)	Median Lead(−) or Lag(+) in Months (10)	Timing Class[b] (11)	% in Timing Class (12)
3. Fixed capital investment											
New investment commitments											
825. New orders, machine tools	P	4	4	0(0)	0	4	0	0	−16	L	100
	T	5	3	2(0)	1	4	1	1	−2	U	
Investment expenditures											
819. Gross private dom. investment, total, Q	P	5	4	4(0)	1	5	0	2	−3	L	80
	T	5	3	2(1)	1	5	0	2	−5	L	60
818. Gross private dom. investment, bus.	P	5	0	4(2)	2	4	1	1	0	C	80
sec., Q	T	5	1	3(1)	2	4	1	1	0	U	
821. Mfrs.' sales, prod. dur. equip., value	P	4	2	2(0)	2	4	0	0	−3	U	
	T	4	0	4(0)	4	4	0	0	+2	Lg	100
820. Index of equipment production	P	4	2	3(2)	0	4	0	0	−1	C	75
	T	4	0	4(0)	4	4	0	0	+1	C	100
822. New construction expend., bus. sec.	P	5	2	2(0)	2	4	1	2	+1	U	
	T	5	0	2(1)	3	4	1	2	+5	Lg	60
4. Inventories and inventory investment											
Inventories											
64. Mfrs.' inventories, total, value	P	8	2	5(0)	6	8	0	0	+2	Lg	75
	T	8	1	4(0)	7	8	0	0	+3	Lg	88
Inventory investment and purchasing											

Series											
Flows of money and credit											
827. New nonfarm mortgages recorded,	P	5	3	0(0)	0	3	2	2	−11	U	
$20,000 and under	T	5	3	0(0)	0	3	2	2	−4	U	
111. Corporate gross savings, Q	P	3	2	2(0)	1	3	0	0	−3	U	
	T	3	2	2(1)	0	3	0	0	−2	L	67
824. Stock offerings, mfg. corp., Q	P	3	3	1(0)	0	3	0	2	−5	L	100
	T	3	1	2(1)	1	3	0	2	0	U	
823. Stock, shares sold, N.Y.S.E.	P	21	17	2(0)	2	19	2	6	−12	L	81
	T	22	15	6(2)	3	20	2	6	−4	L	68
Credit difficulties											
15. No. of bus. failures, liab. $100,000 and	P	17	13	7(2)	2	17	0	2	−5	L	76
over (inv.)	T	18	12	3(0)	5	17	1	2	−6	L	67
828. Delinquency rates, auto direct loans	P	4	4	2(0)	0	4	0	0	−4	L	100
(inv.)	T	4	2	2(0)	2	4	0	0	−2	U	

[a] Rough coincidences include exact coincidences (shown in parentheses) and leads and lags of 3 months or less. Leads (lags) include leads (lags) of 1 month or more. The total number of timing comparisons, which can be less than the number of business cycle turns covered by the series, is the sum of the leads, exact coincidences, and lags. Leads and lags of quarterly series are expressed in terms of months.

[b] The classification for individual series is based on the median lead or lag plus a probability test applied to the number of leads, rough coincidences, or lags relative to the number of business cycle turns covered.

[c] Also analyzed positively, in which case the series is classed as leading.

[d] Earlier segment omitted, 1879–1918 (bank clearings).

[e] Based on fewer than 3 timing comparisons.

Appendix D
Conformity and Timing Scores for 1948–65

Classification and Series Title (1)	Scores: Conformity (2)	Timing (3)	Average Conformity and Timing (4)
LEADING INDICATORS (36 SERIES)			
1. Employment and unemployment			
Marginal employment adjustments			
*1. Avg. workweek, prod. workers, mfg.	88	44	66
*30. Nonagri. placements, BES	72	86	79
2. Accession rate, mfg.	72	81	76
5. Initial claims, unempl. insur. (inv.)	76	52	64
3. Layoff rate, mfg. (inv.)	78	72	75
3. Fixed capital investment			
Formation of business enterprises			
*38. Index of net business formation	90	72	81
13. New business incorporations	52	22	37
New investment commitments			
*6. New orders, dur. goods indus.	72	82	77
94. Construction contracts, total, value	4	20	12
*10. Contracts and orders, plant and equip.	92	50	71
11. New capital appropriations, mfg., Q	76	8	42
24. New orders, mach. and equip. indus.	92	82	87
9. Constr. contracts, comm. and indus., floor area	6	10	8
7. Private nonfarm housing starts	52	80	66
*29. New building permits, private housing units	74	80	77
4. Inventory and inventory investment			
Inventory investment and purchasing			
21. Change in business inventories, all indus., Q	96	48	72
*31. Change in book value, mfg. and trade inventories	76	70	73
37. Purchased materials, % reptg. higher inventories	76	55	66
20. Change in bk. val., mfrs.' inventories of mat. and supp.	56	48	52
26. Buying policy, mater., % reptg. commitments 60+ days	66	71	68
32. Vendor performance, % reptg. slower deliveries	78	82	80
25. Change in unfilled orders, dur. goods indus.	96	79	88
5. Prices, costs, and profits			
Sensitive commodity price indexes			
*23. Industrial materials prices	72	72	72
Stock price indexes			
*19. Stock prices, 500 common stocks	52	86	69
Profits and profit margins			
*16. Corporate profits after taxes, Q	54	72	63
22. Ratio, profits to income orig., corp., all indus., Q	52	72	62
18. Profits per dollar of sales, corporate, mfg., Q	74	72	73
*17. Ratio, price to unit labor cost, mfg.	88	52	70
6. Money and credit			
Flows of money and credit			
98. Change in money supply and time deposits	8	22	15
85. Change in money supply	76	23	50
110. Total private borrowing, Q	88	39	64

Appendix D (*Continued*)

Classification and Series Title (1)	Scores: Conformity (2)	Timing (3)	Average Conformity and Timing (4)
*113. Change in consumer instalment debt	76	48	62
112. Change in bank loans to businesses	76	52	64
33. Change in mortgage debt	54	20	37
Credit difficulties			
14. Liabilities of business failures (inv.)	26	16	21
39. Delinquency rate, instal. loans, 30+ days (inv.)	72	50	61
ROUGHLY COINCIDENT INDICATORS (25 SERIES)			
1. Employment and unemployment			
Job vacancies			
301. Nonagri. job openings, number pending, BES	74	58	66
46. Help-wanted advertising	94	54	74
Comprehensive employment series			
501. Man-hours in nonfarm establishments, employees	88	56	72
*41. Employees in nonagri. establishments	88	90	89
42. Total nonagri. employment	68	43	56
Comprehensive unemployment series			
*43. Unemployment rate, total (inv.)	94	68	81
45. Insured unemployment rate (inv.)	73	76	74
40. Unemployment rate, married males (inv.)	52	38	45
2. Production, income, consumption, and trade			
Comprehensive production series			
49. GNP in current dollars, expenditure estimate, Q	90	59	74
*50. GNP in constant dollars, expenditure estimate, Q	88	80	84
*47. Industrial production	90	49	70
Comprehensive income series			
*52. Personal income	70	28	49
53. Labor income in mining, mfg., and constr.	90	82	86
Comprehensive consumption and trade series			
57. Final sales in current dollars, Q	20	20	20
*816. Mfg. and trade sales	70	80	75
*54. Sales of retail stores	68	14	41
3. Fixed capital investment			
Backlog of investment commitments			
96. Mfrs.' unfilled orders, dur. goods indus.	72	52	62
97. Backlog of cap. appropriations, mfg., Q	74	44	59
5. Prices, costs, and profits			
Comprehensive wholesale price indexes			
55. Wholesale prices exc. farm products and foods	70	20	45
58. Wholesale price index, mfd. goods	2	20	11
6. Money and credit			
Money market interest rates			
114. Treasury bill rate	98	22	60
116. Corporate bond yields	92	19	56
115. Treasury bond yields	92	50	71
117. Municipal bond yields	86	39	62
Bank reserves			
93. Free reserves (inv.)	96	25	60

Appendix D (*Concluded*)

Classification and Series Title (1)	Scores: Conformity (2)	Timing (3)	Average Conformity and Timing (4)
LAGGING INDICATORS (11 SERIES)			
1. Employment and unemployment			
Long-duration unemployment			
*502. Unempl. rate, persons unempl. 15+ weeks (inv.)	98	52	75
3. Fixed capital investment			
Investment expenditures			
*61. Bus. expend., new plant and equip., Q	92	90	91
505. Mach. and equip. sales and bus. constr. expend.	92	58	75
4. Inventories and inventory investment			
Inventories			
*71. Book value, mfg. and trade inventories	90	90	90
65. Book value of mfrs.' inventories, finished goods	90	86	88
5. Prices, costs, and profits			
Unit labor costs			
68. Labor cost per dollar of real corp. GNP, Q	88	56	72
*62. Labor cost per unit of output, mfg.	88	58	73
6. Money and credit			
Outstanding debt			
66. Consumer instalment debt	2	21	12
*72. Comm. and indus. loans outstanding	72	28	50
Interest rates on business loans and mortgages			
*67. Bank rates on short-term bus. loans, Q	84	24	54
118. Mortgage yields, residential	70	24	47

Note: Timing is based on measures that do not necessarily pertain to the same classification as that for the full period.

Appendix E
Median Lead (or Lag) of Seventy-two Selected Indicators Adjusted for Loss of Currency When Smoothed by MCD Moving Averages

Classification and Series Title (1)	Median Lead(−) or Lag(+) at Peaks and Troughs, (Months) (2)	$\bar{I}/\bar{C}$ (3)	MCD Span[a] (Months) (4)	$\bar{I}/\bar{C}$ for MCD Span[a] (5)	Median Lead(−) or Lag(+) Adjusted for MCD Span[b] (Months) (6)
LEADING INDICATORS (36 SERIES)					
1. Employment and unemployment					
Marginal employment adjustments					
*1. Avg. workweek, prod. workers, mfg.	−5	2.23	3	.74	−4
*30. Nonagri. placements, BES	−3	1.23	2	.63	−3
2. Accession rate, mfg.	−4	3.20	4	.84	−3
5. Initial claims, unempl. insur. (inv.)	−6	2.02	2	.95	−6
3. Layoff rate, mfg. (inv.)	−7	2.41	3	.77	−6
3. Fixed capital investment					
Formation of business enterprises					
*38. Index of net business formation	−7	1.15	2	.66	−7
13. New business incorporations	−5	2.18	3	.78	−4
New investment commitments					
*6. New orders, dur. goods indus.	−4	2.20	3	.66	−3
94. Construction contracts, total, value	−6	4.12	5	.87	−4
*10. Contracts and orders, plant and equip.	−6	3.08	4	.84	−5
11. New capital appropriations, mfg., Q	−4	.61	3[f]	.61	−3
24. New orders, mach. and equip. indus.	−6	2.51	3	.88	−5
9. Constr. contracts, comm. and indus., floor area	−2	9.41	10	.94	+2
7. Private nonfarm housing starts	−6	7.91	8	.99	−3
*29. New building permits, private housing units	−6	2.54	3	.80	−5
4. Inventories and inventory investment					
Inventory investment and purchasing					
21. Change in business inventories, all indus., Q	−2	1.00	6[f]	.46	0
*31. Change in book value, mfg. and trade inventories	−8	4.70	5	.98	−6
37. Purchased materials, % reptg. higher inventories	−4	1.85	3	.76	−3
20. Change in bk. val., mfrs.' inventories of mat. and supplies	−6	4.97	6	.96	−4
26. Buying policy, mater., % reptg. commitments 60+ days	−4	2.41	3	.77	−3
32. Vendor performance, % reptg. slower deliveries	−8	1.45	2	.95	−8
25. Change in unfilled orders, dur. goods indus.	−12	3.51	4	.98	−11
5. Prices, costs, and profits					
Sensitive commodity price indexes					
*23. Industrial materials prices	−2	1.41	2	.99	−2
Stock price indexes					
*19. Stock prices, 500 common stocks	−4	1.02	2	.57	−4
Profits and profit margins					
*16. Corporate profits after taxes, Q	−2	.72	3[f]	.72	−1
22. Ratio, profits to income orig., corp., all indus., Q	−7	.92	3[f]	.92	−6

Appendix E (*Continued*)

Classification and Series Title (1)	Median Lead(−) or Lag(+) at Peaks and Troughs, (Months) (2)	$\bar{I}/\bar{C}$ (3)	MCD Span[a] (Months) (4)	$\bar{I}/\bar{C}$ for MCD Span[a] (5)	Median Lead(−) or Lag(+) Adjusted for MCD Span[b] (Months) (6)
LEADING INDICATORS (CONCLUDED)					
18. Profits per dollar of sales, corporate, mfg., Q	−7	.95	3[f]	.95	−6
*17. Ratio, price to unit labor cost, mfg.	−3	1.92	3	.81	−2
6. Money and credit					
Flows of money and credit					
98. Change in money supply and time deposits[c]	−15	8.78	9	.98	−11
85. Change in money supply[c]	−14	10.88	11	.99	−9
110. Total private borrowing, Q	−8	.93	3[f]	.93	−7
*113. Change in consumer instalment debt	−10	2.56	3	.92	−9
112. Change in bank loans to businesses	−4	3.87	5	.95	−2
33. Change in mortgage debt	−8	4.87	5	.88	−6
Credit difficulties					
14. Liabilities of bus. failures (inv.)	−7	10.72	11	.97	−2
39. Delinquency rate, instal. loans, 30+ days (inv.)	−3	2.55	3	.80	−2
ROUGHLY COINCIDENT INDICATORS (25 SERIES)					
1. Employment and unemployment					
Job vacancies					
301. Nonagri. job openings, number pending, BES	0	.78	1	.78	0
46. Help-wanted advertising	0	.81	1	.81	0
Comprehensive employment series					
501. Man-hours in nonfarm establishments, employees	−1	1.23	2	.57	−1
*41. Employees in nonagri. establishments	0	.55	1	.55	0
42. Total nonagri. employment	−2	1.50	2	.80	−2
Comprehensive unemployment series					
*43. Unemployment rate, total (inv.)	0	1.39	2	.72	0
45. Insured unemployment rate (inv.)	0	.67	1	.67	0
40. Unemployment rate, married males (inv.)	−4	1.71	2	.91	−4
2. Production, income, consumption, and trade					
Comprehensive production series					
49. GNP in current dollars, expenditure estimate, Q	0	.25	3[f]	.25	+1
*50. GNP in constant dollars, expenditure estimate, Q	−2	.35	3[f]	.35	−1
*47. Industrial production	0	.71	1	.71	0
Comprehensive income series					
*52. Personal income	−1	.58	1	.58	−1
53. Labor income in mining, mfg., and constr.	0	.82	1	.82	0
Comprehensive consumption and trade series					
*816. Mfg. and trade sales	0	1.22	2	.62	0
57. Final sales in current dollars, Q	+3	.25	3[f]	.25	+4
*54. Sales of retail stores	0	1.67	2	.98	0
3. Fixed capital investment					
Backlog of investment commitments					
96. Mfrs.' unfilled orders, dur. goods indus.	−3	.42	1	.42	−3
97. Backlog of cap. appropriations, mfg., Q	+3	.19	3[f]	.19	+4

Appendix E (*Continued*)

Classification and Number of Series (1)	Median Lead(−) or Lag(+) at Peaks and Troughs, (Months) (2)	$\bar{I}/\bar{C}$ (3)	MCD Span[a] (Months) (4)	$\bar{I}/\bar{C}$ for MCD Span[a] (5)	Median Lead(−) or Lag(+) Adjusted for MCD Span[b] (Months) (6)
ROUGHLY COINCIDENT INDICATORS (CONCLUDED)					
5. Prices, costs, and profits					
Comprehensive wholesale price indexes					
55. Wholesale prices exc. farm products and foods	+1	.71	1	.71	+1
58. Wholesale price index, mfd. goods	0	.91	1	.91	0
6. Money and credit					
Money market interest rates					
114. Treasury bill rate	−1	1.12	2	.73	−1
116. Corporate bond yields	0	2.48	4	.93	+1
115. Treasury bond yields	0	1.41	2	.98	0
117. Municipal bond yields	+2	1.90	3	.87	+3
Bank reserves					
93. Free reserves (inv.)[d]	−1	1.68	3	.68	0
LAGGING INDICATORS (11 SERIES)					
1. Employment and unemployment					
Long-duration unemployment					
*502. Unempl. rate, persons unempl. 15+ weeks (inv.)	+2	1.22	2	.62	+2
3. Fixed capital investment					
Investment expenditures					
*61. Bus. expend., new plant and equip., Q	+1	.26	3[f]	.26	+2
505. Mach. and equip. sales and bus. constr. expend.	+2	1.43	2	.68	+2
4. Inventories and inventory investment					
Inventories					
*71. Book value, mfg. and trade inventories	+2	.41	1	.41	+2
65. Book value of mfrs.' inventories, finished goods	+5	.65	1	.65	+5
5. Prices, costs, and profits					
Unit labor costs					
68. Labor cost per dollar of real corp. GNP, Q[e]	+7	.62	3[f]	.62	+8
*62. Labor cost per unit of output, mfg.[e]	+8	1.28	2	.72	+8
6. Money and credit					
Outstanding debt					
66. Consumer instalment debt	+4	.14	1	.14	+4
*72. Comm. and indus. loans outstanding	+2	.27	1	.27	+2
Interest rates on business loans and mortgages					
*67. Bank rates on short-term bus. loans, Q[e]	+5	.54	3[f]	.54	+6
118. Mortgage yields, residential[e]	+4	.65	1	.65	+4

Appendix E (*Concluded*)

Classification and Number of Series (1)	Median Lead(−) or Lag(+) at Peaks and Troughs, (Months) (2)	Ī/C̄ (3)	MCD Span[a] (Months) (4)	Ī/C̄ for MCD Span[a] (5)	Median Lead(−) or Lag(+) Adjusted for MCD Span[b] (Months) (6)
GROUP SUMMARIES (MEDIANS)					
Leading Indicators	*−6*	*2.41*	*3*	*.88*	*−4*
Marginal employment adjustments (5)	−5	2.23	3	.77	−4
Formation of business enterprises (2)	−6	1.66	2	.72	−6
New investment commitments (8)	−6	2.81	4	.86	−4
Inventory investment and purchasing (7)	−6	2.41	4	.95	−4
Sensitive commodity price indexes (1)	−2	1.41	2	.99	−2
Stock price indexes (1)	−4	1.02	2	.57	−4
Profits and profit margins (4)	−5	.94	3	.86	−4
Flows of money and credit (6)	−9	4.37	5	.94	−8
Credit difficulties (2)	−5	6.64	7	.88	−2
Roughly Coincident Indicators	*0*	*.82*	*2*	*.71*	*0*
Job vacancies (2)	0	.80	1	.80	0
Comprehensive employment series (3)	−1	1.23	2	.57	−1
Comprehensive unemployment series (3)	0	1.39	2	.72	0
Comprehensive production series (3)	0	.35	3	.35	0
Comprehensive income series (2)	0	.70	1	.70	0
Comprehensive consumption and trade series (3)	0	1.22	2	.62	0
Backlog of investment commitments (2)	0	.30	2	.30	0
Comprehensive wholesale price indexes (2)	0	.81	1	.81	0
Money market interest rates (4)	0	1.66	2	.90	0
Bank reserves (1)	−1	1.68	3	.68	0
Lagging indicators	*+4*	*.62*	*2*	*.62*	*+4*
Long-duration unemployment (1)	+2	1.22	2	.62	+2
Investment expenditures (2)	+2	.84	2	.47	+2
Inventories (2)	+4	.53	1	.53	+4
Unit labor costs (2)	+8	.95	2	.67	+8
Outstanding debt (2)	+3	.20	1	.20	+3
Interest rates on business loans and mortgages (2)	+4	.60	2	.60	+5

Note: For periods covered by column 2, which vary from series to series, see Table 6. Period covered by columns 3 to 5 is 1953–65 in most instances.

[a] The MCD span is the shortest-period moving average for which the average month-to-month change in the trend-cycle component is greater than that of the irregular component ($\bar{I}/\bar{C} < 1.00$) and remains so. For MCD spans of 6 months or less, the $\bar{I}/\bar{C}$ ratio in column 5 is computed from the moving average with MCD span. For MCD spans greater than 6 months, the span and the corresponding $\bar{I}/\bar{C}$ ratio are computed by choosing the minimum level of MCD which will, when divided into the $\bar{I}/\bar{C}$ ratio for a one-month span (column 3), reduce the ratio to less than 1.00. The latter method generally yields a close estimate for MCD spans of 6 months or less as well. See *Business Cycle Indicators*, Vol. I, p. 537.

[b] Median lead or lag plus one-half the MCD span, less 0.5 if the MCD span is odd or less 1.0 if the MCD span is even. This is an estimate of what the median lead or lag would be for a moving average of MCD span, after adjustment for loss of currency due to centering of the moving average (at the center of the span if the span is odd, or one-half month later if the span is even).

[c] Also analyzed invertedly, in which case the series is classed as lagging.

[d] Also analyzed positively, in which case the series is classed as lagging.

[e] Also analyzed invertedly, in which case the series is classed as leading.

[f] Quarterly span expressed in months.

Appendix F
Monthly Chronology of Business Cycles in the United States, 1854–1961

Dates of		Duration in Months of			
				Full Cycle	
Trough	Peak	Expansion	Contraction[a]	Trough to Trough	Peak to Peak
December 1854	June 1857	30	18	48	
December 1858	October 1860	22	8	30	40
June 1861	April 1865	46	32	78	54
December 1867	June 1869	18	18	36	50
December 1870	October 1873	34	65	99	52
March 1879	March 1882	36	38	74	101
May 1885	March 1887	22	13	35	60
April 1888	July 1890	27	10	37	40
May 1891	January 1893	20	17	37	30
June 1894	December 1895	18	18	36	35
June 1897	June 1899	24	18	42	42
December 1900	September 1902	21	23	44	39
August 1904	May 1907	33	13	46	56
June 1908	January 1910	19	24	43	32
January 1912	January 1913	12	23	35	36
December 1914	August 1918	44	7	51	67
March 1919	January 1920	10	18	28	17
July 1921	May 1923	22	14	36	40
July 1924	October 1926	27	13	40	41
November 1927	August 1929	21	43	64	34
March 1933	May 1937	50	13	63	93
June 1938	February 1945	80	8	88	93
October 1945	November 1948	37	11	48	45
October 1949	July 1953	45	13	58	56
August 1954	July 1957	35	9	44	48
April 1958	May 1960	25	9	34	34
February 1961					

Note: For the quarterly chronology, 1854–1958, and the annual chronology, 1834–1958, see *Business Cycle Indicators*, Vol. I, p. 670. For 1960–61, the quarterly peak and trough dates are II 1960 and I 1961; the calendar-year peak and trough dates are 1960 and 1961; and the fiscal-year peak and trough dates are the years ending June 30, 1960, and June 30, 1961, respectively.

[a] From peak on same line to trough on next line.

Appendix G
Titles and Sources of Series Reviewed in This Report

Note: The numbers assigned to the series are for identification only and do not reflect relationships among the series. The numbers are given in all text tables and charts as well as in the index. Series preceded by an asterisk are on short list of 25 indicators. Abbreviated names of source agencies are:

BES: Bureau of Employment Security, Department of Labor
BLS: Bureau of Labor Statistics, Department of Labor
Census: Bureau of the Census, Department of Commerce
FRB: Board of Governors of the Federal Reserve System
FHA: Federal Housing Administration
FTC: Federal Trade Commission
NAPA: National Association of Purchasing Agents, Business Survey Committee
NBER: National Bureau of Economic Research
NICB: National Industrial Conference Board
OBE: Office of Business Economics, Department of Commerce
SEC: Securities and Exchange Commission

Series Number and Title	Source (current data shown first, historical segments next)
*1. Average hours of work per week, production workers, manufacturing	BLS, 1935ff.; NICB, 1920–34; seasonal adjustment by NBER for 1920–34
2. Labor turnover, manufacturing, gross accession rate	BLS, June 1929ff.; Metropolitan Life Insurance Co., 1919–May 1929; seasonal adjustment by NBER for 1919–May 1929
3. Labor turnover, manufacturing, total layoff rate	See 2
4. Number of persons on temporary layoff, all industries	BLS and Census, July 1959ff.; Census, 1947–June 1959; seasonal adjustment by Census
5. Initial claims, unemployment insurance, state programs	BES, 1945ff.; seasonal adjustment by Census
*6. Manufacturers' new orders, durable goods industries	Census, 1947ff.; OBE, 1939–46, seasonal adjustment by NBER; NICB, 1929–38; NBER, 1920–29
7. New private nonfarm housing units started, number	Census, 1945ff.; BLS, 1939–44; F. W. Dodge Co. (floor area of residential building contracts awarded), 1918–38; seasonal adjustment of residential contracts by NBER
9. Construction contracts awarded for commercial and industrial buildings, floor area	F. W. Dodge Co., seasonal adjustment by Census, 1960ff., and NBER, 1919–59
*10. Contracts awarded, and orders for plant and equipment, value	F. W. Dodge Co. and Census, 1948ff.; seasonal adjustment by NBER and Census
11. New capital appropriations, 1,000 manufacturing corporations	NICB, 1953ff.
13. Number of new business incorporations	Dun and Bradstreet, Inc., 1945ff.; Corporation Trust Company, 1936–44; G. H. Evans, Jr., *Business Incorporations in the United States, 1800–1943* (NBER, 1948); seasonal adjustment by Census and NBER
14. Liabilities of business failures, all commercial	Dun and Bradstreet, Inc., 1875ff.; seasonal adjustment by Census, 1960ff., and by NBER, 1875–1959
15. Number of business failures with liabilities of $100,000 and over	Dun and Bradstreet, Inc., 1894ff.; seasonal adjustment by Census, 1960ff.; by NBER, 1894–1959. Data represent weekly averages per month of all business failures with over $100,000 liabilities, 1948ff.; through 1947, only monthly failures of manufacturing firms with over $100,000 liabilities were included.
*16. Corporate profits after taxes	OBE, 1939ff.; H. Barger, *Outlay and Income in the United States, 1921–1938* (NBER, 1942)

Appendix G (*Continued*)

Series Number and Title	Source (current data shown first, historical segments next)
*17. Price per unit of labor cost index: ratio, index of wholesale prices of manufactured goods to index of total labor cost (production worker wage cost prior to 1948) per unit of output in manufacturing	BLS; OBE; and FRB, 1948ff., seasonal adjustment by Census; same sources for 1919–48 data except for segment of wholesale price index by F. C. Mills which comes from unpublished table, 1941ff., and from *Prices in a War Economy* (NBER, 1943), 1927–40; seasonal adjustment of production worker wage cost, 1919–48, by NBER
18. Profits (before taxes) per dollar of sales, all manufacturing corporations	FTC and SEC, 1947ff.; seasonal adjustment by Census
*19. Index of stock prices, 500 common stocks	Standard and Poor's Corp., 1918ff.; Cowles Commission for Research in Economics, 1871–1917
20. Change in book value, manufacturers' inventories of purchased materials	OBE, 1939–61 (discontinued); current estimates of inventories of materials and supplies by Census available from 1953 on
21. Change in business inventories, all industries	OBE, 1939ff.; H. Barger, *op. cit.*, 1921–38
22. Ratio of profits (after taxes) to income originating, corporate, all industries	OBE, 1946ff.
*23. Index of industrial materials prices	BLS, 1935ff.; unpublished index compiled by R. P. Mack (NBER), described in "Inflation and Quasi-Elective Changes in Costs," *Review of Economics and Statistics*, August 1959, 1919–34
24. Manufacturers' new orders, machinery and equipment industries	Census, 1948ff.
25. Change in manufacturers' unfilled orders, durable goods industries	Census, 1947ff.; OBE, 1939–46
26. Members' buying policy, percentage reporting commitments for production materials, 60 days or longer	NAPA, 1950ff.
*29. New private housing units authorized by local building permits	Census, 1946ff.; index based on Census estimates, 1954ff., and on BLS estimates, 1946–53, seasonal adjustment by Census; F. W. Dodge Co. (floor area of residential building contracts awarded), 1918–45; seasonal adjustment by NBER
*30. Nonagricultural placements, all industries	BES, 1945ff.; seasonal adjustment by Census
*31. Change in book value of manufacturing and trade inventories	Census and OBE, 1939ff.
32. Vendor performance: percentage of members reporting slower deliveries	Purchasing Agents Association of Chicago, 1946ff.
33. Change in mortgage debt held by financial institutions and life insurance companies	Federal Home Loan Bank Board; National Association of Mutual Savings Banks; FRB; and Institute of Life Insurance, 1955ff.; seasonal adjustment by Census
37. Percentage of members reporting higher inventories of purchased materials	NAPA, 1947ff.; seasonal adjustment by Census
*38. Index of net business formation	Dun and Bradstreet, Inc., and Census, 1948ff.; seasonal adjustment by Census and NBER; OBE, 1945–47
39. Consumer instalment loans, delinquency rate, 30 days and over	American Bankers Association, Instalment Credit Commission, 1947ff.; seasonal adjustment by NBER. Number of delinquent loans as percentage of total number outstanding.
40. Unemployment rate, married males, spouse present	BLS and Census, July 1959ff.; Census, 1954–June 1959; seasonal adjustment by BLS

Appendix G (*Continued*)

Series Number and Title	Source (current data shown first, historical segments next)
*41. Employees in nonagricultural establishments	BLS, 1929ff.; seasonal adjustment prior to 1939 by FRB
42. Total nonagricultural employment	BLS and Census, July 1959ff.; Census, 1940–June 1959; seasonal adjustment by NBER prior to 1947
*43. Unemployment rate, total	BLS and Census, July 1959ff.; Census, May 1940–June 1959; NICB, 1929–April 1940; seasonal adjustment, 1948ff., by BLS; 1929–47, by NBER
45. Average weekly insured unemployment rate, state programs	BES, 1949ff.
46. Index of help-wanted advertising in newspapers	NICB, 1951ff.; Metropolitan Life Insurance Co., 1919–50; seasonal adjustment, 1919–50, by NBER
*47. Index of industrial production	FRB, 1919ff.
49. Gross national product in current dollars, expenditure estimate	OBE, 1939ff.; H. Barger and L. R. Klein, unpublished estimates, revising figures in H. Barger, *op. cit.*, 1921–38
*50. Gross national product in constant dollars, expenditure estimate	OBE, 1947ff.; H. Barger and L. R. Klein, unpublished estimates, revising figures in H. Barger, *op. cit.*, 1921–38
51. Bank debits outside New York City	FRB, 1919ff.; seasonal and working day adjustments by NBER (series represents 343 banking centers, April 1955–1964; 344 centers, 1943–March 1955; 140 centers, 1919–42; discontinued 1964 and replaced by series covering 224 Standard Metropolitan Statistical Areas, which include all centers formerly covered)
*52. Personal income	OBE, 1929ff.; H. Barger and L. R. Klein, unpublished estimates, revising figures in H. Barger, *op. cit.*, 1921–38
53. Labor income in mining, manufacturing, and construction	OBE, 1929ff.
*54. Sales of retail stores	Census, 1951ff.; OBE, 1935–50; FRB, 1919–34 (index of department store sales)
55. Index of wholesale prices, all commodities other than farm products and foods	BLS, 1913ff.; seasonal adjustment by Census, 1948ff.; by NBER, 1913–47
56. Wholesale trade sales	Census (merchant wholesalers), 1948ff.; OBE (total wholesale trade), 1939–47; FRB (index of wholesale trade sales in 9 lines), 1919–29
57. Final sales in current dollars	OBE, 1939ff.; H. Barger, *op. cit.*, 1921–38
58. Index of wholesale prices of manufactured goods	BLS, 1913ff.; seasonal adjustment by Census, 1947ff.; index of wholesale prices of finished products used 1913–46, no seasonal adjustment for that period
*61. Business expenditures on new plant and equipment, total	OBE and SEC, 1947ff.; L. J. Chawner (Department of Commerce), "Capital Expenditures for Manufacturing Plant and Equipment" (*Survey of Current Business*, March 1941), 1915–40
*62. Index of total labor cost (production worker wage cost prior to 1948) per unit of output	OBE (total employee compensation in manufacturing) and FRB (output in manufacturing), 1948ff.; seasonal adjustment by Census; BLS (production worker payroll in manufacturing) and FRB (output in manufacturing), 1919–48
64. Book value of manufacturers' inventories, total	Census, 1947ff.; OBE, 1926–46
65. Book value of manufacturers' inventories, finished goods	Census, 1953ff.; OBE, 1939–52
66. Consumer instalment debt	FRB, 1929ff.; seasonally adjusted net debt change used to derive seasonally adjusted debt outstanding; prior to February 1955, seasonal adjustment of debt outstanding by NBER

Appendix G (*Continued*)

Series Number and Title	Source (current data shown first, historical segments next)
*67. Bank rates on short-term business loans (customers other than business included, 1919–39)	FRB, 1939ff.; FRB (unpublished data), 1929–39; W. W. Riefler (FRB), *Money Rates and Money Markets in the United States* (1930), 1919–28
68. Index of labor cost per dollar of real corporate gross product (ratio: compensation of corporation employees to value of corporate product in 1958 dollars)	OBE and Census, 1948ff.
*71. Book value of manufacturing and trade inventories, total	Census and OBE, 1939ff.
*72. Commercial and industrial bank loans outstanding	FRB, 1937ff.; seasonal adjustment by NBER. Data represent commercial and industrial loans outstanding on last Wednesday of month as reported by member banks in leading cities through June 29, 1966, and by large commercial banks thereafter.
81. Index of consumer prices, all items	BLS, 1913ff.; seasonal adjustment by Census, 1947ff.; by NBER, 1913–33
82. Federal expenditures: cash payments to the public, 1948ff.; budget expenditures, 1879–1948	Bureau of Accounts, Treasury Department, and Bureau of the Budget, 1948ff.; seasonal adjustment by Census; Treasury Department, Fiscal Service, and predecessor agencies, 1879–1948; seasonal adjustment by NBER
83. Federal receipts: cash receipts from the public, 1948ff.; budget receipts, 1879–1948	See 82
84. Federal surplus or deficit: cash, 1948ff.; budget, 1879–1948	See 82
85. Percentage change in total money supply (demand deposits plus currency)	FRB, 1947ff.; M. Friedman and A. J. Schwartz, *A Monetary History of the United States: 1867–1960* (Princeton University Press for NBER, 1963), 1907–46
86. Total exports (excluding military aid shipments after June 1950)	Census, and predecessor agencies, 1866ff.; seasonal adjustment by Census, 1948ff.; by NBER, 1866–1947
87. General imports, total	See 86
88. Merchandise trade balance	See 86
89. Excess of receipts or payments in the U.S. balance of payments	OBE, 1945ff., seasonal adjustment by NBER, 1945–49
90. Defense Department obligations, procurement	Department of Defense, Fiscal Analysis Division, 1953ff. seasonal adjustment by Census
91. Defense Department obligations, total	See 90
92. Military prime contract awards to U.S. business firms	Department of Defense, Directorate for Statistical Services, 1951ff.; seasonal adjustment by Census
93. Free reserves at Federal Reserve Banks (member banks' excess reserves minus borrowings)	FRB, 1929ff.
94. Construction contracts awarded, total, value	F. W. Dodge Co., 1910ff.; seasonal adjustment by NBER
95. Federal surplus or deficit on national income and product accounts	OBE, 1946ff.
96. Manufacturers' unfilled orders, durable goods industries	Census, 1947ff.; OBE, 1939–46; seasonal adjustment, 1939–46, by NBER
97. Backlog of capital appropriations, 1,000 manufacturing corporations	NICB, 1953ff.
98. Percentage change in total money supply plus commercial bank time deposits	See 85
99. Manufacturers' new orders, defense products	Census, 1953ff.
101. Federal purchases of goods and services, national defense	OBE, 1946ff.

Appendix G (*Continued*)

Series Number and Title	Source (current data shown first, historical segments next)
110. Total private borrowing by nonfinancial borrowers	FRB, 1952ff.
111. Corporate gross savings	FRB, 1952ff. (gross retained earnings of non-financial corporations)
112. Change in bank loans to businesses	FRB, 1937ff.; seasonal adjustment by NBER; see 72
*113. Net change in consumer instalment debt	FRB, 1929ff.; prior to 1955, seasonal adjustment by NBER (month-to-month change in seasonally adjusted debt outstanding at end of month)
114. Treasury bill rate, new issues, 3-month bills	FRB, 1920ff.; yield on 3–6-month Treasury notes and certificates used 1920–30; seasonal adjustment by NBER, 1948–61, and 1920–30
115. Yield on long-term Treasury bonds	Treasury Department, 1919ff.
116. Yield on new issues of high-grade corporate bonds	Treasury Department, 1960ff.; First National City Bank, 1948–59
117. Yield on high-grade municipal bonds	*The Bond Buyer*, 1948ff.; Standard and Poor's Corp., 1919–48
118. Secondary market yields on FHA-insured home mortgages for immediate delivery	FHA, 1964ff.; S. A. Klaman (National Association of Mutual Savings Banks, unpublished estimates), 1953–63; J. M. Guttentag (unpublished estimates made for Federal Reserve Bank of New York), 1948–53
301. Nonagricultural job openings, number pending	BES, 1946ff.; seasonal adjustment by Census
501. Man-hours in nonfarm establishments, all employees	BLS and Census, July 1959ff.; Census for workweek component and BLS for employment, 1941–June 1959; seasonal adjustment by Census
*502. Unemployment rate, percentage of persons unemployed 15 weeks and over	BLS and Census, July 1959ff.; Census, 1948–June 1959; seasonal adjustment by BLS
503. Manufacturers' sales, total	Census, 1947ff.; OBE, 1926–46
505. Manufacturers' sales of machinery and equipment, and business construction expenditures	Census, 1953ff. (machinery and equipment sales) and 1948ff. (business construction expenditures); OBE, 1948–52 (unpublished estimates of machinery and equipment sales)
801. Man-hours in nonfarm industries, persons with a job	BLS and Census, July 1959ff.; Census, 1941–June 1959; seasonal and holiday adjustments by NBER
802. Man-hours in nonfarm industries, persons at work	See 801
803. Unemployment rate, percentage of persons unemployed less than 5 weeks	BLS and Census, July 1959ff.; Census, 1948–June 1959; seasonal adjustment by BLS
804. Unemployment rate, percentage of persons unemployed 5 to 14 weeks	See 803
805. Labor turnover rate, manufacturing, new hires	BLS and BES, 1951ff. (series is component of accession rate)
806. Labor turnover rate, manufacturing, rehires	See 805
807. Nonagricultural employment, commodity-producing industries	BLS, 1939ff.
808. Nonagricultural employment, service industries	See 807
809. Help-wanted display ads for executive positions in newspapers, total	Beveridge Organization, Chicago, Ill., for Heidrick and Struggles, Chicago-Los Angeles, 1954ff.; seasonal adjustment by NBER
810. Gross national product in current dollars, income estimate	OBE, 1939ff. (gross national product or expenditure minus "statistical discrepancy")

Appendix G (*Concluded*)

Series Number and Title	Source (current data shown first, historical segments next)
811. Gross national product in constant dollars, income estimate	See 810 (implicit price deflator applied to series 810)
812. Final sales in constant dollars	OB , 1947ff.
813. Automobile production, passenger cars	FRB (index of production of autos, based on *Ward's Automotive Reports*), 1947ff., Census, July 1921–1941, and National Automobile Chamber of Commerce, 1913–June 1921 (factory sales of passenger cars); seasonal adjustment for 1913–41 by NBER
814. Steel ingot production	American Iron and Steel Institute, July 1917ff.; *Iron Age*, 1899–June 1917, seasonal adjustment by NBER
815. Index of truck tonnage hauled	American Trucking Associations, Department of Research and Transportation Economics, 1946ff.
*816. Manufacturing and trade sales	Census and OBE, 1946ff.
817. Personal consumption expenditures, durable goods	OBE, 1939ff.
818. Gross private domestic investment, business sector	See 819 (aggregate investment in producers' durable equipment and nonresidential structures, prior to 1946, construction was represented by new construction, excluding residential nonfarm)
819. Gross private domestic investment, total	OBE 1939ff.
820. Index of production of equipment, including defense	FRB, 1947ff.
821. Manufacturers' sales of machinery and equipment	Census, 1953ff., OBE (unpublished estimates), 1948–52
822. New construction expenditures, business sector	Census, 1939ff. (aggregate value in current dollars of industrial, commercial, and public utility construction put in place)
823. Number of shares sold on the New York Stock Exchange	*Commercial and Financial Chronicle* and New York Stock Exchange, 1875ff.
824. Common stock offerings, manufacturing corporations	SEC, 1951; seasonal adjustment by NBER (estimated gross proceeds of all new common stock offered for cash sale)
825. Metal cutting type machine tools, domestic gross new orders	National Machine Tool Builders' Association, 1945ff.; seasonal adjustment by NBER
826. Month-to-month change in department store stocks on hand and on order	FRB, 1940–63, seasonal adjustment by NBER
827. New nonfarm mortgages recorded, $20,000 and under	Federal Home Loan Bank Board, 1939–65, seasonal adjustment by NBER
828. Automobile direct instalment loans, delinquency rate, 30 days and over	American Bankers Association, Instalment Credit Commission, 1947ff.; seasonal adjustment by NBER. Number of delinquent loans as percentage of total outstanding
861. Manufacturers' new orders for exports of durable goods, excluding motor vehicles and parts	Census, 1962ff.
862. Index of new machinery orders for export, McGraw-Hill	McGraw-Hill Publishing Co., 1957ff., seasonal adjustment by NBER

Index

Entries in **boldface** type refer to tables. Series numbers (shown in parentheses) are for identification only and do not reflect series relationships or order.